The
Airdrop Bible

The Ultimate Guide to Earning Passive Income through Airdrops ...

Henry Otasowere

The Airdrop Bible

©Copyright 2023 Henry Otasowere, " The Airdrop Bible: *"The Ultimate Guide to Earning Passive Income through Airdrops "*

ALL RIGHTS RESERVED

No part of this publication may be reproduced, stored in a retrieval system, or transmitted, in any form or by any means, electronic, mechanical, photocopying, recording or otherwise, without the express written permission of the author.

Printed by:

Otimage Publishers

Printed in the United States of America

First Printing Edition, 2023

Paper Cover - **ISBN: 9798385613519**

CONTENTS

Introduction 5
What are airdrops? 8
Why participate in airdrops? 11
How much can you earn from airdrops? 16
Who is this book for? 21
Part 1 1
Airdrops 101 1
    Chapter **1** 2
    Airdrops 101 2
What are airdrops? 4
    Chapter **2** 7
    Why do companies offer airdrops? 7
    Chapter **3** 11
    Types of airdrops 11
Bounty Airdrops 14
Holder Airdrops 16
Fork Airdrops 18
Snapshot Airdrops 20
    Chapter **4** 24
    The history of airdrops 24
Part 2 28
Getting Started with Airdrops 28
    Chapter **5** 29
    Getting Started with Airdrops 29
How to find airdrops 32
How to register for airdrops 33
Wallets and exchanges for airdrops 35
Claiming tokens 36
Airdrop eligibility requirements 39
How to maximize your chances of getting airdropped tokens 40
Part 3 43
Participating in Airdrops 43
    Chapter **6** 44
    Participating in Airdrops 44
What to do after you receive an airdrop 46
How to claim airdropped tokens 47
How to store airdropped tokens 49

How to sell or trade airdropped tokens 53
Tax considerations for airdrops 55
Part 4 58
Airdrop Platforms 58
    Chapter 7 59
    Airdrop Platforms 59
Best platforms for finding airdrops 61
Platform reviews and comparisons 62
How to spot fake airdrop platforms 64
How to avoid scams 65
Part 5 68
    Chapter 8 69
    Advanced Airdrop Strategies 69
Airdrop Arbitrage 73
Airdrop Farming 75
Token Swapping 76
    Chapter 9 79
    How to create your own airdrops 79
How to participate in bounty programs 81
How to use airdrops for marketing 83
How to invest in airdrop projects 85

Introduction

Welcome to "The Airdrop Bible: The Ultimate Guide to Earning Passive Income through Airdrops." If you're new to the world of cryptocurrency, you may be wondering what exactly airdrops are and how they can help you earn passive income. Airdrops are a powerful tool for crypto companies to raise awareness, grow their user base, and reward loyal supporters with free tokens.

This book is a comprehensive guide for beginners on how to leverage the power of airdrops to earn passive income. We'll cover everything you need to know to get started with airdrops, from what they are and why they matter, to how to participate in them, which platforms to use, and how to avoid scams.

We'll start by laying the foundation for what airdrops are and how they work, including their history and future outlook. We'll then dive into the practical aspects of finding and participating in airdrops, including how to register for airdrops, which wallets and exchanges to use, and how to maximize your chances of getting airdropped tokens.

We'll also review the best platforms for finding airdrops and how to avoid scams, as well as advanced strategies for creating your own airdrops, participating in bounty programs, using airdrops for marketing, and investing in airdrop projects.

By the end of this book, you'll have a deep understanding of how airdrops work and how to use them to your advantage. Whether you're a crypto enthusiast looking to earn some extra income or an entrepreneur looking to leverage airdrops for your own projects, "The Airdrop Bible" has got you covered. Let's dive in!

In this book, we'll take you on a journey through the exciting world of airdrops, where you'll learn how to navigate the often confusing and complex landscape of cryptocurrency. We'll demystify the process of finding and participating in airdrops, so you can start earning passive income with ease.

But we won't stop at the basics. We'll also cover advanced strategies for using airdrops to grow your crypto portfolio, as well as how to use airdrops for marketing and investment purposes. And we'll provide you with valuable insights into how to spot fake airdrop platforms and avoid scams.

"The Airdrop Bible" is the only book you'll need to master the art of earning passive income through airdrops. We've drawn on our extensive experience in the crypto industry to bring you a comprehensive and up-to-date guide that covers everything you need to know.

So whether you're a complete beginner or an experienced crypto trader, this book is for you. Get ready to unlock the power of airdrops and take your crypto earnings to the next level!

Our goal with "The Airdrop Bible" is to provide you with a comprehensive resource that will help you understand the world of airdrops and how to leverage them for passive income. We'll guide you through every step of the process, from understanding the basics of airdrops to advanced strategies for creating your own airdrops and investing in airdrop projects.

We believe that airdrops are one of the most exciting and innovative ways to earn passive income in the cryptocurrency space. But we also recognize that the world of airdrops can be confusing and overwhelming, especially for beginners.

That's why we've written this book in a clear and concise manner, using simple language and real-world examples to help you understand complex concepts. We want you to feel empowered and confident in your ability to participate in airdrops and earn passive income.

We've also included practical tips and advice throughout the book, based on our own experiences and those of other successful airdrop participants. We've learned from our mistakes and want to help you avoid common pitfalls and scams.

So if you're ready to take your crypto earnings to the next level and earn passive income through airdrops, "The Airdrop Bible" is the perfect guide for you. Let's get started!

What are airdrops?

Airdrops are a way for cryptocurrency projects to distribute free tokens to their community, either as a reward for supporting the project or as a way to promote their platform. Airdrops can be a great way for individuals to get involved with new projects and earn some extra income without having to invest any of their own money.

However, many people may not realize that not all airdrops are created equal. Some airdrops may be scams or fraudulent, designed to trick people into giving away their personal information or access to their crypto wallets. It's important to carefully research any airdrop project before participating, to ensure that it's legitimate and safe.

Additionally, many people may not realize that there are different types of airdrops. Some airdrops may require participants to complete certain tasks or meet certain criteria, such as holding a certain amount of a specific cryptocurrency. Other airdrops may be open to anyone who signs up, without any specific requirements.

Another important aspect of airdrops is that they are often time-limited, meaning that participants need to act quickly in order to take advantage of them. Airdrops may only be available for a limited period of time, or may have a limited number of tokens available, so it's important to stay up-to-date on the latest airdrop opportunities and act quickly when they arise.

Overall, while airdrops can be a great way to earn passive income in the crypto space, it's important to be aware of the potential risks and pitfalls. By doing your research, staying informed, and acting quickly when opportunities arise, you can take advantage of the many benefits of airdrops while minimizing your risk.

Another thing that many people may not know about airdrops is that they can be a valuable marketing tool for cryptocurrency projects.

Airdrops can help to raise awareness of a new project, attract new users and investors, and build a community around a platform.

By distributing free tokens to users, airdrops can incentivize people to get involved with a project and become early adopters. This can be especially valuable for new or relatively unknown projects that are looking to build momentum and gain traction in the competitive crypto space.

Airdrops can also be a way for cryptocurrency projects to distribute their tokens in a more decentralized and equitable way. By distributing tokens through airdrops, projects can ensure that their tokens are held by a diverse group of users, rather than just a small group of early investors.

However, it's important to be aware that not all airdrops are genuine or worthwhile. Some airdrops may be scams or fraudulent, designed to trick people into giving away their personal information or access to their crypto wallets. It's essential to carefully research any airdrop project before participating, to ensure that it's legitimate and safe.

Overall, airdrops can be a valuable way to earn passive income, get involved with new crypto projects, and support the growth of the crypto ecosystem. By staying informed, doing your research, and taking advantage of legitimate opportunities, you can make the most of this exciting and innovative way to earn crypto.

Another important aspect of airdrops that many people may not be aware of is that they can be a way to diversify your cryptocurrency holdings. By participating in airdrops, you can earn tokens for a variety of different projects, which can help you to spread out your crypto investments and reduce your overall risk.

Additionally, some airdrops may be for projects that are not yet listed on major exchanges, meaning that the only way to get access to their tokens is through the airdrop. By participating in these early-stage airdrops, you may be able to get in on the ground floor of a promising project, potentially earning significant returns down the line.

However, it's important to be aware that not all airdrops are worthwhile, and some may not be worth the time and effort required to participate. It's important to carefully research any airdrop project before participating, to ensure that it's legitimate and has potential for long-term growth.

Overall, airdrops can be a valuable tool for diversifying your crypto holdings and getting involved with new projects. By staying informed, doing your research, and taking advantage of legitimate opportunities, you can make the most of this exciting and innovative way to earn passive income in the crypto space.

Why participate in airdrops?

Participating in airdrops can offer several benefits beyond just earning free tokens. Here are some reasons why you may want to participate in airdrops:

Get involved with new projects: Airdrops can be an excellent way to discover and get involved with new crypto projects. By participating in airdrops, you can learn about different platforms and technologies, and potentially find new investment opportunities.

Earn passive income: Airdrops can be a great way to earn passive income in the crypto space, without having to invest any of your own money. By completing simple tasks or meeting certain criteria, you can earn free tokens that may increase in value over time.

Diversify your portfolio: By participating in airdrops, you can earn tokens for a variety of different projects, which can help you to spread out your crypto investments and reduce your overall risk.

Support the growth of the crypto ecosystem: By participating in legitimate airdrops, you can help to support the growth and adoption of the crypto ecosystem. Airdrops can help to attract new users and investors to different projects, and can help to build communities around different platforms.

Access early-stage projects: Some airdrops may be for projects that are not yet listed on major exchanges, meaning that the only way to get access to their tokens is through the airdrop. By participating in these early-stage airdrops, you may be able to get in on the ground floor of a promising project, potentially earning significant returns down the line.

However, it's important to be aware that not all airdrops are worthwhile, and some may not be worth the time and effort required to participate. It's essential to carefully research any airdrop project before participating, to ensure that it's legitimate and has potential for long-term growth.

Overall, participating in airdrops can be a valuable way to get involved with new projects, earn passive income, and support the growth of the crypto ecosystem. By staying informed, doing your research, and taking advantage of legitimate opportunities, you can make the most of this exciting and innovative way to earn crypto.

Another benefit of participating in airdrops is that it can help you to learn about different aspects of the crypto space. For example, many airdrops require you to complete certain tasks or meet certain criteria, such as following a project on social media or joining a Telegram group. By completing these tasks, you can learn more about different platforms and technologies, as well as the communities that are built around them.

Participating in airdrops can also be a way to network with other people in the crypto community. By joining Telegram groups or other online communities for different projects, you can connect with other investors and enthusiasts who share your interests. This can be a valuable way to learn more about different projects, as well as to get advice and insights from other experienced investors.

Finally, participating in airdrops can be a way to have some fun in the crypto space. Many airdrops are designed to be engaging and interactive, with tasks that are both challenging and rewarding. By participating in these airdrops, you can have a bit of fun while also potentially earning some free tokens.

However, as mentioned earlier, it's important to be careful when participating in airdrops. There are many scams and fraudulent projects in the crypto space, and it can be difficult to tell the legitimate opportunities from the fake ones. Always do your research and look for reputable projects with strong teams and clear roadmaps. By doing so, you can ensure that your time and effort are well spent, and that you're participating in airdrops that have the potential to generate real value over time.

Another important point to consider when participating in airdrops is the potential tax implications. Depending on where you live, earning free tokens through airdrops may be considered taxable income. It's important to consult with a tax professional to understand the tax laws in your jurisdiction and to ensure that you are properly reporting any income from airdrops on your tax returns.

Additionally, it's important to note that not all airdrops are created equal. Some airdrops may offer only a small number of tokens or may have strict requirements for participation, while others may offer significant rewards for relatively easy tasks. It's important to carefully evaluate each airdrop opportunity to determine whether the potential rewards are worth the time and effort required.

Finally, it's important to be mindful of the potential risks associated with participating in airdrops. In addition to the risk of scams and fraudulent projects, there is also the risk of losing money if the value of the tokens you earn through airdrops decreases over time. It's important to carefully evaluate each project and to consider factors such as the project's technology, team, and long-term potential before deciding whether to participate in an airdrop.

In summary, participating in airdrops can be a valuable way to earn passive income, support the growth of the crypto ecosystem, and learn more about different platforms and technologies. However, it's important to carefully evaluate each airdrop opportunity to ensure that it's legitimate and has the potential to generate real value over time. By doing so, you can make the most of this exciting and innovative way to earn crypto.

One thing that many people may not realize is that participating in airdrops can also be a way to support the growth and development of different crypto projects. By participating in an airdrop, you are helping to increase awareness of the project and its goals, which can in turn attract more investors and supporters.

In some cases, participating in airdrops may even be a way to support charitable causes or social initiatives. For example, some airdrops may require participants to make a donation to a charitable organization or to engage in social activism in order to earn tokens. By participating in these airdrops, you can support important causes while also potentially earning some free tokens.

Another important aspect of participating in airdrops is the potential for long-term gains. While the tokens earned through airdrops may not have significant value initially, they may increase in value over time as the project grows and gains more users and investors. By holding onto these tokens and participating in the project's ecosystem, you may be able to realize significant gains over the long term.

Ultimately, participating in airdrops can be a fun and rewarding way to earn passive income and learn more about the crypto space. However, it's important to approach each airdrop opportunity with caution and to carefully evaluate the potential risks and rewards before deciding whether to participate. By doing so, you can make the most of this exciting opportunity and potentially earn some free tokens in the process.

Another potential benefit of participating in airdrops is the opportunity to diversify your crypto portfolio. By participating in airdrops for a variety of projects and platforms, you can accumulate a diverse range of tokens without having to make any financial investments. This can be a valuable strategy for those who are new to crypto or who have limited resources to invest in the market.

Furthermore, participating in airdrops can also be a way to learn more about different crypto projects and technologies. By participating in an airdrop, you may be required to engage with the project's community, learn about its technology, or use its platform. This can be a valuable learning experience and can help you to better understand the strengths and weaknesses of different projects and platforms.

Finally, participating in airdrops can be a way to build relationships within the crypto community. By participating in an airdrop, you may have the opportunity to connect with other investors, traders, and enthusiasts who share your interests and goals. This can lead to valuable networking opportunities, as well as the potential for future collaborations or partnerships.

Overall, participating in airdrops can be a valuable way to earn passive income, support the growth of the crypto ecosystem, diversify your portfolio, learn more about different projects and technologies, and build relationships within the community. While there are certainly risks associated with participating in airdrops, by approaching each opportunity with caution and careful evaluation, you can potentially reap significant rewards over the long term.

One additional aspect of airdrops that many people may not consider is the potential for creating new use cases for tokens. Airdrops can be a way for projects to distribute their tokens to a wider audience and encourage adoption of their platform or technology. By distributing tokens to participants who have a vested interest in the success of the project, the project can potentially build a strong community of supporters who are more likely to use the tokens for their intended purpose.

In addition to creating new use cases for tokens, airdrops can also help to increase liquidity for the project's tokens. By distributing tokens to a wider audience, the project can potentially increase trading volumes and liquidity on exchanges, which can help to drive up the value of the tokens over time.

Finally, participating in airdrops can be a way to stay up to date with the latest trends and developments in the crypto space. As new projects and technologies emerge, participating in their airdrops can be a way to stay on the cutting edge and gain early access to potentially valuable tokens.

In summary, participating in airdrops can be a valuable way to support the growth of different crypto projects, diversify your portfolio, learn more about different projects and technologies, build relationships within the community, create new use cases for tokens, increase liquidity, and stay up to date with the latest trends and developments in the crypto space. While there are certainly risks associated with participating in airdrops, by carefully evaluating each opportunity and taking appropriate precautions, you can potentially reap significant rewards over the long term.

How much can you earn from airdrops?

The amount that you can earn from airdrops can vary widely depending on a number of factors, including the platform, the token being distributed, and the specific terms of the airdrop. In some cases, airdrops may only provide a small amount of tokens, while in other cases, they may provide a more substantial amount. Additionally, the value of the tokens that you receive from airdrops can fluctuate widely over time, making it difficult to predict exactly how much you can earn.

One factor that many people may not be aware of when it comes to airdrops is the potential for additional rewards beyond the initial token distribution. In some cases, projects may offer additional incentives for users to hold or stake the tokens that they receive from the airdrop. These incentives may include additional tokens or rewards, or access to exclusive features or services on the platform.

Another factor to consider when evaluating the potential earnings from airdrops is the long-term potential for the tokens that you receive. While the immediate value of the tokens may be relatively small, if the project behind the tokens is successful, the value of the tokens could increase significantly over time. This can potentially lead to significant earnings for those who hold onto the tokens over the long term.

Finally, it's important to consider the potential risks associated with participating in airdrops. While there is certainly the potential for significant earnings, there is also the risk of scams or fraudulent projects that may distribute tokens with no real value or potential. Additionally, participating in airdrops can be time-consuming and may require significant effort to navigate the various platforms and processes involved.

Overall, while the earnings potential from airdrops can be difficult to predict, it's important to carefully evaluate each opportunity and consider the long-term potential for the tokens being distributed.

Additionally, taking appropriate precautions to avoid scams and fraudulent projects is essential to ensure that you are not putting your funds or personal information at risk.

It's also important to consider the tax implications of participating in airdrops. In some cases, the tokens received from airdrops may be considered taxable income by the relevant tax authorities. This means that you may be required to report the value of the tokens as income and pay taxes on that amount. Additionally, if you sell the tokens at a later date, you may be required to pay capital gains taxes on any profits.

Another factor to consider is the potential impact of airdrops on the wider crypto ecosystem. While airdrops can be a valuable way to distribute tokens and encourage adoption of new projects, they can also contribute to token dilution and create market saturation. This can potentially lead to a situation where the value of individual tokens is diminished due to oversupply, which can negatively impact the long-term potential for earnings from airdrops.

Finally, it's worth noting that the landscape of airdrops is constantly evolving, with new platforms and projects emerging on a regular basis. This means that it's important to stay up to date with the latest trends and developments in the space in order to maximize your earnings potential. This may involve following industry publications and forums, as well as networking with other participants in the space to learn about new opportunities and best practices for participating in airdrops.

In conclusion, while the earnings potential from airdrops can vary widely depending on a number of factors, they can be a valuable way to earn passive income and support the growth of different crypto projects. By carefully evaluating each opportunity and taking appropriate precautions, you can potentially reap significant rewards over the long term. Additionally, by staying up to date with the latest trends and developments in the space, you can position yourself for continued success in the world of airdrops and beyond.

One important factor to keep in mind when considering how much you can earn from airdrops is the impact of competition. As more and more people participate in airdrops, the value of the tokens being distributed may decrease due to oversupply. This means that it may become more difficult to earn substantial amounts of income from airdrops as time goes on.

Another key consideration when evaluating the potential earnings from airdrops is the level of effort required to participate. While some airdrops may be relatively easy to participate in and require minimal effort, others may be more complex and time-consuming. This may involve completing various tasks or activities on social media platforms, engaging with other members of the community, or even contributing to the development of the project in some way.

It's also important to be aware of the potential risks associated with participating in airdrops. In addition to the risk of scams and fraudulent projects, there is also the risk of losing funds due to market fluctuations or the failure of the project behind the tokens being distributed. This means that it's important to carefully evaluate each opportunity and consider the potential risks and rewards before committing your time and resources to any particular airdrop.

Finally, it's worth noting that there are a number of strategies that you can use to maximize your earnings potential from airdrops. This may include participating in a variety of different airdrops, diversifying your portfolio of tokens, and holding onto tokens for the long term in order to benefit from potential future growth. By taking a strategic approach to airdrops and carefully evaluating each opportunity, you can potentially earn significant passive income and support the growth of the wider crypto ecosystem.

It's also worth noting that there are different types of airdrops, and the potential earnings from each type can vary widely. Some airdrops may distribute tokens to a large number of participants, but the value of each token may be relatively low. Other airdrops may distribute a smaller number of tokens to a smaller group of participants, but the value of each token may be much higher. Additionally, some airdrops may offer additional rewards or incentives for completing certain tasks or activities, such as sharing information about the project on social media or referring other users to the project.

In addition to evaluating the potential earnings from each airdrop, it's important to consider the long-term potential of the project behind the tokens being distributed. Airdrops can be a valuable way to support the growth of new crypto projects and help to increase their adoption and visibility. By participating in airdrops for promising new projects, you can potentially benefit from the growth of the project over the long term, which may result in increased earnings and profits.

Finally, it's important to consider the broader context of the crypto ecosystem when evaluating the potential earnings from airdrops. While airdrops can be a valuable way to earn passive income, they are just one aspect of the broader crypto landscape. It's important to have a well-rounded understanding of the market and the various opportunities available in order to maximize your earnings potential and make informed investment decisions.

Overall, the potential earnings from airdrops can vary widely depending on a number of factors, including the type of airdrop, the level of competition, the effort required to participate, and the long-term potential of the project behind the tokens being distributed. By carefully evaluating each opportunity and taking appropriate precautions, you can potentially earn significant passive income and support the growth of the wider crypto ecosystem.

Another factor to consider when evaluating the potential earnings from airdrops is the timing of your participation. Airdrops can be highly competitive, and the early bird often gets the worm. Some airdrops may offer higher rewards to participants who sign up early, while others may have a limited number of tokens available to distribute. This means that it's important to stay up to date on the latest airdrop opportunities and act quickly in order to maximize your potential earnings.

Additionally, it's important to keep in mind that airdrops can be subject to market volatility. The value of the tokens being distributed can fluctuate based on a number of factors, including market demand, supply and demand dynamics, and overall market conditions. This means that the value of your earnings from airdrops can also fluctuate over time. However, if you believe in the long-term potential of the project behind the tokens being distributed, then you may be willing to hold onto the tokens and wait for the market to recover.

Another important consideration is the tax implications of earning passive income from airdrops. Depending on where you live, you may be required to pay taxes on your earnings from airdrops. It's important to consult with a tax professional or accountant in order to understand your obligations and ensure that you are in compliance with local tax laws.

Overall, while airdrops can be a valuable way to earn passive income and support the growth of the crypto ecosystem, it's important to carefully evaluate each opportunity and consider the potential risks and rewards. By staying informed, taking appropriate precautions, and acting quickly to capitalize on opportunities, you can potentially earn significant passive income from airdrops and contribute to the growth and development of the wider crypto ecosystem.

Who is this book for?

This book is designed for anyone who is interested in earning passive income through airdrops, regardless of their level of experience with cryptocurrency or blockchain technology. While some knowledge of crypto basics may be helpful, the book is written in a beginner-friendly style that assumes no prior knowledge.

However, what many people may not know is that airdrops are not just for seasoned crypto investors or enthusiasts. In fact, airdrops can be a valuable way for anyone to dip their toes into the world of cryptocurrency and start earning passive income with minimal risk or upfront investment.

For example, if you're new to the world of cryptocurrency and don't have any funds to invest, participating in airdrops can be a great way to start accumulating tokens and building your portfolio. By participating in airdrops, you can earn tokens for free or with minimal effort, which can then be traded or held as a long-term investment.

Additionally, airdrops can be a valuable tool for diversifying your investment portfolio and reducing your overall risk. By participating in a variety of airdrops across different projects and platforms, you can spread your risk and potentially benefit from the growth of multiple projects over time.

Finally, this book is also for anyone who is interested in learning more about the broader crypto ecosystem and the various opportunities available for earning passive income. While airdrops are just one aspect of the wider crypto landscape, they can be a valuable way to support the growth of the ecosystem and potentially earn significant returns over time.

Overall, this book is designed for anyone who is interested in earning passive income through airdrops, regardless of their level of experience or background. Whether you're a seasoned investor or a crypto newbie, this book will provide you with the knowledge, tools, and strategies you need to start earning passive income through airdrops and contribute to the growth and development of the wider crypto ecosystem.

It's important to note that this book is not just for individuals who are interested in earning passive income through airdrops. The book is also for those who want to learn more about the crypto ecosystem and the potential of blockchain technology. Airdrops are just one aspect of the wider crypto landscape, and by learning about airdrops, readers can gain a deeper understanding of how blockchain technology is disrupting traditional industries and creating new opportunities for innovation and growth.

Additionally, this book is for individuals who want to take control of their financial future and explore new ways to generate passive income. Airdrops are just one of many potential avenues for earning passive income, but they can be a valuable tool for diversifying your portfolio and potentially earning significant returns over time. By learning about airdrops and the various strategies and tools available for participating in them, readers can gain the knowledge and confidence they need to start building their own passive income streams.

Finally, this book is for individuals who are passionate about supporting the growth and development of the wider crypto ecosystem. Airdrops are a powerful way to incentivize community participation and reward individuals for contributing to the growth and success of a project. By participating in airdrops, readers can support the development of innovative new projects and help to build a more decentralized and equitable financial system.

Overall, this book is for anyone who wants to learn more about the potential of blockchain technology, explore new ways to generate passive income, and contribute to the growth and development of the wider crypto ecosystem. By reading this book and applying the strategies and tools outlined within, readers can potentially earn significant passive income through airdrops and help to shape the future of finance.

PART 1
Airdrops 101

CHAPTER 1
AIRDROPS 101

When it comes to understanding airdrops, there are a few key concepts that many people may not be familiar with.

Airdrops 101 is a comprehensive guide to understanding these concepts and gaining a deeper understanding of how airdrops work.

One important concept to understand is the difference between an airdrop and a bounty program. While both of these programs involve earning tokens or coins for completing certain tasks, there are some key differences between the two. Airdrops are typically distributed for free to a large number of users, while bounty programs are often more targeted and involve completing specific tasks, such as promoting a project on social media or creating content. Understanding the differences between these programs can help readers determine which opportunities are the best fit for their skills and interests.

Another key concept to understand is the role of wallets in participating in airdrops. Airdrops are often distributed directly to users' wallets, which means that having a compatible wallet is essential for participating in these programs. Different projects may require different types of wallets, and understanding how to set up and use these wallets can be a crucial part of participating in airdrops.

It's also important to understand the different types of airdrops that exist. While most airdrops involve receiving tokens or coins for free, there are some variations on this model, such as airdrops that require users to hold a certain amount of tokens or coins in order to receive additional rewards. Understanding the different types of airdrops and the requirements for participating in each one can help readers make informed decisions about which programs to participate in.

Finally, it's important to understand the potential risks and downsides of participating in airdrops. While airdrops can be a valuable way to earn passive income and support the growth of new projects, there are also risks involved, such as scams, fraud, and market volatility. Understanding these risks and taking steps to mitigate them can help readers participate in airdrops safely and effectively.

Overall, Airdrops 101 is a comprehensive guide to understanding the basics of airdrops and gaining a deeper understanding of how these programs work. By mastering these key concepts and understanding the risks and rewards of participating in airdrops, readers can potentially earn significant passive income and support the growth of the wider crypto ecosystem.

In addition to the key concepts outlined above, there are some other important considerations to keep in mind when participating in airdrops. One of these is the importance of timing. Airdrops can be announced and distributed at any time, so it's important to stay up-to-date with news and announcements from projects that interest you. Being able to participate in an airdrop early can be crucial for maximizing the potential rewards.

Another important consideration is the role of social media in airdrops. Many projects use social media platforms like Twitter and Telegram to announce and distribute airdrops, so it's important to follow these channels and stay active in the communities. Engaging with other users and promoting projects can also increase the chances of receiving additional rewards or participating in future airdrops.

It's also important to understand the potential tax implications of participating in airdrops. Depending on your jurisdiction and the specifics of the airdrop program, you may be required to report any income earned from airdrops on your tax returns. Understanding these requirements and seeking professional advice if necessary can help avoid potential legal issues down the line.

Finally, it's worth noting that airdrops are just one potential avenue for earning passive income in the crypto space. There are a variety of other opportunities available, such as staking, yield farming, and liquidity provision. Understanding the differences between these programs and choosing the ones that best fit your skills and interests can help you maximize your earnings and support the growth of the wider crypto ecosystem.

Another important aspect to consider when participating in airdrops is the security of your crypto assets. Since airdrops often require you to disclose your public wallet address, it's crucial to ensure that you are using a secure wallet that you control the private keys to. This can help protect your assets from hacks and scams.

It's also important to be aware of the potential for scams and phishing attacks related to airdrops. Bad actors may try to impersonate legitimate projects and offer fake airdrops in an attempt to steal users' funds. Always be cautious and do your due diligence before participating in any airdrop program.

Furthermore, it's important to understand the potential risks associated with participating in airdrops. Airdrops are typically used as a marketing tool by projects to build community engagement and attract new users. While the potential rewards can be significant, the value of airdropped tokens can also be highly volatile and subject to market fluctuations.

As with any investment or income-generating activity, it's important to approach airdrops with a realistic and informed mindset. Understanding the risks and potential rewards, doing your research, and diversifying your portfolio can help you make the most of this exciting opportunity to earn passive income in the crypto space.

What are airdrops?

Airdrops are a popular marketing technique used by blockchain-based projects to attract new users and build community engagement. In an airdrop, a project distributes a certain amount of its tokens or cryptocurrency to a large number of individuals for free, usually in exchange for completing certain tasks or meeting certain criteria.

However, there are some aspects of airdrops that many people may not be aware of. For example, while some airdrops are distributed automatically to all holders of a certain cryptocurrency, others may require you to actively participate by completing tasks such as following the project on social media, joining their Telegram group, or referring new users.

Additionally, some airdrops may require you to meet certain eligibility criteria, such as being a resident of a certain country or holding a certain amount of a specific cryptocurrency. It's important to carefully read the terms and conditions of each airdrop before participating to ensure that you are eligible and that you understand the requirements.

Another aspect that some people may not be aware of is the potential value of airdropped tokens. While the initial value of airdropped tokens can vary widely depending on the project, they can potentially increase in value over time as the project gains popularity and adoption. Some airdrops have led to significant gains for participants, but it's important to remember that there are no guarantees and that the value of airdropped tokens can also be highly volatile.

Lastly, it's important to be aware of the potential for scams and phishing attacks related to airdrops. Bad actors may try to impersonate legitimate projects and offer fake airdrops in an attempt to steal users' funds. Always be cautious and do your due diligence before participating in any airdrop program.

Another aspect of airdrops that many people may not know of is the potential for different types of tokens to be distributed. While most airdrops distribute tokens from the project itself, some airdrops may distribute tokens from other projects that are affiliated with or partnered with the airdrop project. These tokens may have their own unique use cases and value propositions.

It's also worth noting that airdrops can take various forms beyond just distributing tokens. Some airdrops may offer other types of rewards, such as discounts on products or services offered by the project, access to exclusive content or events, or even a share in the project's revenue.

Moreover, airdrops can also serve as a way to spread awareness and adoption of new blockchain technology. By distributing tokens or rewards for completing certain tasks, airdrops incentivize users to become more familiar with blockchain technology and its potential applications.

Finally, it's important to remember that not all airdrops are created equal. Some projects may offer airdrops as a genuine way to attract new users and build community engagement, while others may use airdrops as a way to artificially inflate their token's value or as a means to conduct fraudulent activities. Always do your research and carefully evaluate each airdrop before participating to ensure that it is legitimate and aligned with your investment goals.

CHAPTER 2
WHY DO COMPANIES OFFER AIRDROPS?

There are a variety of reasons why companies offer airdrops, beyond just generating buzz and interest in their project. One key reason is to distribute their tokens more widely and fairly, rather than concentrating them in the hands of a few investors or whales. Airdrops allow projects to distribute tokens to a larger and more diverse group of potential users and investors, which can help to build a stronger and more decentralized community around the project.

In addition, airdrops can also serve as a way to incentivize certain behaviors or actions from users. For example, a project may offer airdrops to users who complete certain tasks, such as filling out a survey or joining a Telegram group. This can help to build engagement and participation in the project's community and ecosystem.

Another benefit of airdrops is that they can help to build awareness and adoption of a project among potential users and investors. By offering free tokens or rewards, airdrops can attract more attention and interest in a project than traditional marketing efforts alone. This can help to build a strong and dedicated user base that is invested in the success of the project.

Finally, airdrops can also be used as a way to bootstrap liquidity and trading volume for a new token. By distributing tokens to a large and diverse group of users, airdrops can help to create a more active market for the token, which can help to increase its value and liquidity over time.

Overall, while airdrops are often seen as a marketing gimmick, they can serve a variety of important functions for blockchain projects beyond just generating buzz and hype.

Another key reason why companies offer airdrops is to build trust and credibility among potential users and investors. In the often crowded and competitive blockchain space, building trust and legitimacy can be a major challenge for new projects. By offering airdrops, companies can demonstrate their commitment to transparency, fairness, and community engagement, which can help to build trust and credibility among potential users and investors.

Airdrops can also be a way for projects to reward early supporters and adopters who believe in their vision and mission. By offering free tokens or rewards to early supporters, projects can incentivize them to hold and use their tokens, which can help to build a stronger and more dedicated community around the project.

Another important benefit of airdrops is that they can help to democratize access to new and emerging blockchain projects. In traditional finance, early access to new investment opportunities is often limited to wealthy or well-connected individuals and institutions. By contrast, airdrops allow anyone with an internet connection and a wallet to participate in new and emerging projects, regardless of their background or financial status.

Finally, airdrops can also serve as a way to generate buzz and interest in a project's ecosystem or platform, beyond just its native token. For example, a project may offer airdrops of tokens that are designed to be used for specific purposes within its ecosystem, such as governance or utility tokens. By distributing these tokens to a wider audience, projects can build interest and engagement in their broader ecosystem, which can help to drive adoption and usage over time.

A lesser-known benefit of airdrops is that they can help to address issues of wealth inequality in the crypto space. In traditional finance, wealth inequality is often perpetuated by limited access to investment opportunities and financial resources. By contrast, airdrops allow anyone with an internet connection to participate in new and emerging projects and potentially earn rewards, regardless of their financial status or investment experience.

Furthermore, airdrops can also help to promote decentralization and community ownership within the crypto space. By distributing tokens or rewards to a wider audience, projects can help to ensure that their networks and ecosystems are not dominated by a small group of insiders or early investors. Instead, airdrops can encourage broader community participation and ownership, which can help to promote a more decentralized and democratic ecosystem over time.

Another interesting aspect of airdrops is that they can sometimes be used to incentivize specific behaviors or actions within a project's ecosystem. For example, a project may offer airdrops to users who provide liquidity to a decentralized exchange or who participate in a specific governance vote. By incentivizing these behaviors, projects can help to build more active and engaged communities, which can ultimately help to drive the success and adoption of their platforms.

Finally, it's worth noting that airdrops are not without their risks and challenges. As we've mentioned, scams and frauds are common in the crypto space, and airdrops are no exception. In addition, airdrops can sometimes lead to market saturation and token devaluation if too many tokens are distributed too quickly. As such, it's important for anyone considering participating in airdrops to do their research, stay vigilant for scams, and be mindful of the potential risks and challenges involved.

One thing that many people may not realize is that airdrops can also be a valuable marketing tool for crypto projects. By distributing tokens or rewards to a wide audience, projects can help to raise awareness of their platforms and generate buzz and interest within the crypto community. This can be especially valuable for new and emerging projects that are looking to build a user base and gain traction in the market.

Additionally, airdrops can also help to build brand loyalty and community engagement. By offering rewards and incentives to users who hold and use their tokens, projects can help to build a committed and enthusiastic user base that is more likely to promote and advocate for their platform. This can be especially important in a competitive and rapidly-evolving market like the crypto space, where user loyalty and engagement can be key factors in a project's success.

Finally, it's worth noting that airdrops can also be a valuable tool for fundraising and capital generation. By distributing tokens or rewards to users, projects can help to raise capital and generate liquidity for their platforms. This can be especially useful for early-stage projects that may have difficulty raising capital through traditional fundraising channels. By offering airdrops to users, these projects can help to generate interest and investment in their platforms, which can ultimately help to drive their success and growth over time.

In conclusion, airdrops are a unique and powerful tool in the crypto space that offer a wide range of benefits for users and projects alike. By participating in airdrops, users can earn passive income, gain exposure to new and emerging projects, and potentially help to promote decentralization and community ownership within the crypto ecosystem. At the same time, projects can use airdrops as a marketing tool, a means of building brand loyalty and community engagement, and a fundraising mechanism to help drive their success and growth over time.

CHAPTER 3
TYPES OF AIRDROPS

There are several different types of airdrops in the crypto world, each with its own unique characteristics and benefits. Here are some of the most common types of airdrops:

Standard Airdrops: This is the most common type of airdrop, in which a project distributes free tokens or coins to a large group of users. Standard airdrops are typically used as a marketing tool to help raise awareness of a project and generate interest in its token or coin.

Standard airdrops are the most common type of airdrop, and they are usually done to promote a new cryptocurrency or blockchain project. With standard airdrops, users are given a certain number of tokens for free, simply for completing certain tasks or meeting certain requirements.

Some of the most common tasks that users are asked to complete in order to receive a standard airdrop include following a project's social media accounts, joining their Telegram group, retweeting a tweet, or referring friends to the project. These tasks are designed to help promote the project and build up its community of supporters.

One thing that many people might not be aware of is that standard airdrops can also be used as a way to distribute tokens fairly and evenly among a large group of users. By distributing tokens in this way, developers can ensure that the project's tokens are distributed in a decentralized and democratic manner, rather than being concentrated in the hands of a few early investors.

It's also worth noting that standard airdrops can be a great way for users to learn about new blockchain projects and cryptocurrencies. By participating in airdrops, users can get early access to new tokens and projects, and they can often get a sense of what these projects are all about before deciding whether or not to invest in them.

Overall, standard airdrops are a powerful marketing tool for blockchain projects, and they are a great way for users to get involved in the blockchain ecosystem and learn about new projects and cryptocurrencies. By understanding how standard airdrops work and how to participate in them, users can take advantage of these opportunities to grow their crypto portfolios and become more knowledgeable about the industry as a whole.

Another important aspect of standard airdrops is that they can help projects build a strong community of early adopters and supporters. By offering tokens for completing certain tasks or meeting certain requirements, developers can attract a large and engaged group of users who are interested in the project and its goals.

This early community can be critical for the success of a new blockchain project, as these early adopters can help spread the word about the project, offer feedback and suggestions, and even contribute to the development of the project itself. In many cases, these early adopters can become some of the project's most loyal and dedicated supporters, helping to drive its growth and success over the long term.

It's also worth noting that standard airdrops can vary widely in terms of the amount and value of tokens that are distributed. Some airdrops may offer just a few tokens for completing simple tasks, while others may offer much larger amounts of tokens for more complex or time-consuming tasks.

For users, this means that it's important to carefully evaluate each airdrop opportunity and consider factors such as the value of the tokens being offered, the complexity of the tasks involved, and the reputation of the project offering the airdrop. By doing so, users can ensure that they are making the most of their time and efforts, and that they are participating in airdrops that have the potential to offer real value over the long term.

One potential drawback of standard airdrops is that they can sometimes attract participants who are only interested in the free tokens, rather than the underlying project or its goals. This can lead to a large number of inactive or disengaged users who may not contribute much to the community or the success of the project.

To address this issue, some developers have started to implement more complex airdrop models that require users to demonstrate a deeper understanding or commitment to the project before receiving any tokens. For example, some projects may require users to pass a quiz or complete a tutorial on the project's goals and technology before receiving any tokens.

Other projects may require users to hold a certain amount of a specific token or participate in other activities related to the project, such as staking or liquidity provision, in order to be eligible for airdropped tokens. These more complex models can help to ensure that airdrop recipients are genuinely interested in the project and its goals, and are more likely to become active and engaged members of the community.

Overall, standard airdrops remain an important tool for blockchain projects to attract new users and build a strong community of early adopters. By carefully evaluating each airdrop opportunity and considering factors such as the value of the tokens being offered and the reputation of the project, users can make the most of these opportunities and potentially earn significant rewards over the long term.

In addition to these more complex models, some projects have also begun to experiment with innovative new forms of airdrops that go beyond simply distributing free tokens. For example, some projects may offer airdrops in the form of NFTs (non-fungible tokens), which can represent unique digital assets such as artwork or collectibles.

Other projects may offer airdrops as part of a broader gamification or incentivization program, which can encourage users to participate in various activities and earn rewards based on their contributions to the project. For example, a project might offer a series of airdrops to users who participate in a community vote, write a blog post about the project, or refer new users to the platform.

By leveraging these more innovative airdrop models, projects can not only attract new users and build a strong community, but also promote engagement and participation among their existing user base. This can help to create a more vibrant and active ecosystem around the project, and ultimately increase its chances of long-term success.

Overall, while standard airdrops remain a popular and effective way for blockchain projects to attract new users and build a community, developers are increasingly exploring more complex and innovative models to ensure that airdrop recipients are genuinely interested in the project and its goals. By staying informed about these trends and taking advantage of airdrop opportunities that align with their interests and goals, users can potentially earn significant rewards while supporting the growth and development of the blockchain ecosystem as a whole.

Bounty Airdrops

Bounty airdrops are similar to standard airdrops, but with an added incentive for users to perform certain tasks, such as sharing information about the project on social media, joining a Telegram group, or writing a blog post about the project. Bounty airdrops can help to generate more buzz and engagement around a project, as users are incentivized to actively participate in its promotion.

Bounty airdrops are a specific type of airdrop that involves incentivizing users to perform specific actions or tasks in exchange for tokens. These actions can include anything from joining a project's social media channels, creating content or marketing materials, or even developing code for the project.

In a bounty airdrop, users are typically rewarded with tokens based on the difficulty and impact of the task they complete. For example, a project may offer a larger reward for users who create high-quality marketing materials or develop new features for the platform, while smaller rewards may be offered for simpler tasks such as following the project on social media or referring new users to the platform.

One advantage of bounty airdrops is that they can help projects to build a strong community of dedicated supporters who are willing to actively contribute to the project's growth and development. By incentivizing users to perform specific tasks and rewarding them for their efforts, projects can build a more engaged and active user base, which can help to increase adoption and usage of the platform over time.

However, it is important to note that participating in bounty airdrops can be time-consuming and may require a certain level of expertise or skills. In addition, users should always be careful to only participate in bounty programs from reputable and trustworthy projects, as there have been instances of fraudulent or scam projects using bounty programs to defraud users.

Overall, bounty airdrops can be an effective way for users to earn tokens while contributing to the growth and development of a blockchain project. However, users should carefully consider the requirements and potential risks of each bounty program before participating, and only participate in programs from projects that they trust and believe in.

Types of bounties: Bounty airdrops can have different types of tasks that participants need to complete in order to earn rewards. Some common tasks include social media promotion, content creation, bug reporting, and community engagement. The rewards for each task can vary depending on the difficulty and effort required.

Importance of reading the rules: Bounty airdrops often have specific rules and guidelines that participants need to follow in order to be eligible for rewards. It is important to carefully read and understand these rules before participating, as failing to follow them can result in disqualification and loss of rewards.

Quality over quantity: When participating in a bounty airdrop, it is important to focus on quality over quantity. Rather than trying to complete as many tasks as possible, it is better to focus on a few high-quality tasks that showcase your skills and abilities. This can help you stand out from other participants and increase your chances of earning higher rewards.

Timing is key: Bounty airdrops often have a limited timeframe, so it is important to stay up to date on the latest announcements and complete tasks in a timely manner. Early participation can also be advantageous, as rewards may decrease as more people participate.

Avoid scams: As with any type of airdrop, bounty airdrops can also be a target for scams. It is important to do your own research and verify the legitimacy of the project before participating. Never provide personal or sensitive information, and be wary of offers that seem too good to be true.

Bounty airdrops are a type of airdrop that require participants to complete certain tasks in order to receive their rewards. These tasks can vary widely and may include activities such as social media posts, content creation, bug reporting, translation, and more.

One thing many people may not know about bounty airdrops is that they are often targeted towards specific user groups, such as developers or content creators. This means that if you have certain skills or expertise, you may be able to find bounty airdrops that are better suited to your abilities and offer higher rewards.

Another thing to note is that bounty airdrops typically have a longer duration than standard airdrops, sometimes lasting several weeks or even months. This is because participants need time to complete the required tasks and for the company to review and verify their submissions.

It's also worth mentioning that bounty airdrops often have a higher potential payout than standard airdrops, as the rewards are typically distributed among a smaller group of participants who have completed specific tasks. However, they can also be more competitive and require more effort than standard airdrops, so it's important to carefully evaluate whether a bounty airdrop is worth your time and energy.

Holder Airdrops

Holder airdrops are designed to reward users who hold a certain amount of a project's token or coin in their wallets. These types of airdrops are often used to incentivize long-term holding and discourage selling, which can help to stabilize the token or coin's price and create a more committed user base.

Holder airdrops are another type of airdrop that is becoming increasingly popular in the cryptocurrency space. As the name suggests, holder airdrops reward users simply for holding a particular cryptocurrency in their wallets for a specified period of time.

One thing many people may not know about holder airdrops is that they are often used as a way to incentivize long-term investment in a particular cryptocurrency. By rewarding users for holding onto their coins, companies hope to increase demand for their cryptocurrency and boost its overall value.

Holder airdrops are also a way for companies to distribute their cryptocurrency to a wider audience. By rewarding holders, they can encourage more people to acquire and hold their cryptocurrency, which can help to increase its overall liquidity and trading volume.

It's worth noting that holder airdrops may have specific requirements or restrictions, such as a minimum amount of cryptocurrency that must be held in order to qualify for the reward. Additionally, some holder airdrops may require users to hold their coins for an extended period of time, such as several months or even years, in order to receive the full reward.

Overall, holder airdrops can be a great way for cryptocurrency users to earn passive income and increase their investment portfolio. However, it's important to carefully research the cryptocurrency and company behind the airdrop before investing, as with any investment opportunity.

Holder airdrops are a type of airdrop that rewards users based on the amount of a particular cryptocurrency they hold in their wallets. This means that the more of a specific cryptocurrency a user holds, the more tokens they receive in the airdrop.

Holder airdrops are usually announced in advance and users are given a timeframe in which to hold the specified cryptocurrency in their wallets to be eligible for the airdrop. These airdrops are usually announced by newer projects looking to create a community around their token and incentivize users to hold their tokens for a longer period.

One thing that many people may not know about holder airdrops is that they can be an effective way to promote long-term holding of a particular cryptocurrency. By incentivizing users to hold the cryptocurrency for a longer period, holder airdrops can increase demand for the token, which can lead to higher prices.

Another thing to keep in mind with holder airdrops is that some projects may require users to hold their tokens for a specific amount of time to be eligible for the airdrop. Users who do not meet this requirement may not be eligible for the airdrop, so it's essential to read the terms and conditions carefully.

Overall, holder airdrops can be an excellent way to earn passive income for cryptocurrency holders who are willing to hold a particular token for a more extended period. However, it's essential to do your research and understand the risks and potential rewards before participating in any holder airdrops.

Fork Airdrops

Fork airdrops occur when a blockchain project splits into two separate chains, resulting in users receiving an equal amount of tokens or coins on both chains. This type of airdrop is usually associated with major upgrades or changes to a project's technology or governance structure.

A fork airdrop occurs when a cryptocurrency project creates a new blockchain based on the code of an existing project, with modifications or improvements to the original code. The new blockchain is essentially a copy of the original blockchain, but with some changes that differentiate it from the original project.

When a fork airdrop happens, holders of the original project's tokens or coins are often eligible to receive a certain amount of the new project's tokens for free. This is because the new project wants to attract holders of the original project's tokens to its platform and increase its user base.

One thing that many people may not know about fork airdrops is that they can sometimes be contentious. This is because the creation of a new blockchain based on an existing project's code can be seen as an attempt to compete with or undermine the original project. In some cases, a fork airdrop may be associated with a "hard fork" in which the original project's blockchain is split into two separate blockchains, each with its own set of rules and protocols.

It's also worth noting that not all fork airdrops are created equal. Some forked projects may be more legitimate and successful than others, and some may be outright scams. As with any airdrop or cryptocurrency investment, it's important to do your research and exercise caution before investing time or money into a fork airdrop.

They are based on blockchain forks: Fork airdrops occur when a blockchain undergoes a hard fork, which creates a new chain and token. In some cases, holders of the original token can receive a certain amount of the new token as a form of airdrop.

They can be unpredictable: Fork airdrops are typically not announced in advance, and their timing and mechanics can be unpredictable. This means that investors need to be aware of potential forks in advance and stay informed about any new developments.

They may require action: Unlike some other types of airdrops, fork airdrops may require token holders to take specific actions to receive the new token. This could include setting up a new wallet, registering with a new exchange, or taking other steps to prove ownership of the original token.

They can be valuable: In some cases, fork airdrops can be highly valuable, especially if the new token gains significant traction in the market. However, there are also risks involved, as the value of the new token may be highly volatile and difficult to predict.

They are not without controversy: Forks and fork airdrops have been the subject of controversy in the cryptocurrency community, with some arguing that they are a legitimate way to innovate and improve existing blockchains, while others see them as a way for developers to profit at the expense of existing investors.

Event Airdrops

Event airdrops are tied to specific events or milestones in a project's development or launch, such as a product release or partnership announcement. These types of airdrops can help to generate excitement and interest around a project's progress, as well as reward early adopters and supporters.

Event airdrops are another type of airdrop that is becoming increasingly popular in the cryptocurrency world. These airdrops are specifically designed to reward users for participating in events or promotions hosted by a particular company or project.

The events can take many forms, including participating in a survey, attending a webinar, referring friends, or engaging in social media campaigns. In exchange for these actions, users can receive a reward in the form of tokens or coins.

Event airdrops offer several benefits for both the company and the user. For the company, it is a way to create buzz around their project, generate engagement, and attract new users. For users, it provides an opportunity to earn tokens without having to invest any money.

However, it is important to note that event airdrops often come with certain conditions or requirements that must be met before the reward can be claimed. These requirements can include completing a certain number of actions, meeting certain criteria, or even being one of the first users to participate.

Overall, event airdrops can be a great way to earn tokens while also participating in exciting events and promotions. By keeping an eye out for these opportunities and taking advantage of them, users can increase their chances of earning passive income through airdrops.

Event airdrops are a type of airdrop where users are rewarded for participating in a particular event. These events can include things like attending a conference or meetup, completing a survey, or sharing a social media post about the project.

One thing that many people may not know about event airdrops is that they can be highly targeted towards specific audiences. For example, a blockchain project might hold an event specifically for developers, and offer airdrops to those who attend in order to encourage them to build on their platform. Alternatively, a project might hold an event for their most active community members, and offer airdrops to reward their participation and loyalty.

Another thing to note is that event airdrops can often have strict requirements for participation, such as being physically present at an event or completing a certain task. This means that they may not be as accessible as other types of airdrops, but can offer higher rewards for those who are able to participate.

Overall, event airdrops can be a great way for projects to engage with their community and incentivize participation, while also rewarding users for their time and effort.

Snapshot Airdrops

Snapshot airdrops occur when a project takes a "snapshot" of its blockchain at a specific time and rewards users based on their holdings at that moment. This type of airdrop is often used as a way to distribute tokens or coins to a project's early adopters or long-term holders.

Snapshot airdrops are a type of airdrop that are based on a snapshot of an existing blockchain. Specifically, they reward existing holders of a particular cryptocurrency with a new token, which is usually created as a result of a hard fork or a new blockchain launch. The snapshot is taken at a specific block height or time, and those who hold the specified cryptocurrency at that moment are eligible to receive the new tokens.

One thing that many people do not know about snapshot airdrops is that they can be very lucrative if the new token gains value in the market. For example, if you hold 1,000 units of a cryptocurrency at the time of a snapshot, and you receive 1,000 units of a new token in the airdrop, then you effectively have doubled your holdings. If the new token then appreciates in value, your initial investment could turn into a substantial profit.

Another important point to note about snapshot airdrops is that they are not always announced in advance. This means that you need to be vigilant about news and announcements in the crypto community in order to take advantage of them. Additionally, some snapshot airdrops may require you to hold a minimum amount of the specified cryptocurrency in order to be eligible, so it's important to do your research and understand the rules and requirements of each airdrop.

Snapshot airdrops are a type of airdrop where the distribution of tokens is based on a snapshot of a blockchain at a specific time and date. A snapshot is essentially a record of all the wallet addresses and their token balances on a blockchain at a particular moment in time. The airdrop then distributes tokens to all the wallet addresses that hold a specific cryptocurrency at the time of the snapshot.

The advantage of snapshot airdrops is that they are relatively easy to execute, as they do not require any action on the part of the recipient other than holding the relevant cryptocurrency in their wallet at the time of the snapshot. This makes them a popular choice for blockchain projects that want to distribute tokens to a large number of users without incurring high costs.

However, one of the downsides of snapshot airdrops is that they are often announced with little notice, which can make it difficult for users to prepare and participate. Additionally, the value of the airdropped tokens may not be known at the time of the snapshot, which can make it difficult for users to determine whether it is worth participating in the airdrop.

Overall, snapshot airdrops can be a lucrative way to earn free tokens, but it's important to be aware of the potential risks and challenges associated with them.

It's worth noting that there are many other types of airdrops that can be used in different situations and for different purposes. By understanding the different types of airdrops and their benefits, users can more effectively participate in and benefit from these unique opportunities in the crypto space.

In addition to the traditional airdrop types mentioned earlier, there are some other variations that many people might not be aware of. One such variation is the "staking airdrop," which requires users to hold a certain amount of a particular cryptocurrency in their wallets to be eligible for the airdrop. This type of airdrop is often used to incentivize users to hold a particular cryptocurrency and keep it off the market for a certain period of time.

Another variation is the "bounty airdrop," which involves completing certain tasks or activities in exchange for receiving the airdropped tokens. These tasks can include anything from joining a social media group, retweeting a specific tweet, or even creating content related to the project.

There are also "referral airdrops," where users can earn additional tokens by referring their friends or contacts to participate in the airdrop. In this case, both the referrer and the person they referred can receive tokens, providing an additional incentive to spread the word about the airdrop.

Overall, these variations in airdrop types provide companies with more flexibility in how they distribute tokens and can offer additional benefits to users who participate.

Another type of airdrop that many people might not be aware of is the "airdrop forks." This occurs when a new cryptocurrency project is created by copying the existing code of an established cryptocurrency and making some modifications to it. The new project will often airdrop a new cryptocurrency to holders of the original cryptocurrency, in proportion to the amount they hold. This can be a way for users to receive a new cryptocurrency for free, as long as they hold the original one at the time of the fork.

There are also "ICO airdrops" where a company conducting an initial coin offering (ICO) may offer airdropped tokens as a bonus for investing in their project. In this case, the tokens are not distributed for free, but are instead given as a reward for purchasing a certain amount of tokens during the ICO.

It's also worth noting that some airdrops can come with conditions attached, such as holding the tokens for a certain period of time before being able to sell them. This is often done to encourage users to hold the tokens and prevent them from immediately selling them on the market.

Overall, there are many different types of airdrops, each with its own unique characteristics and benefits. By understanding the various types of airdrops, users can be better equipped to participate in them and maximize their rewards.

Chapter 4
The History of Airdrops

Airdrops have become increasingly popular in recent years, but the concept of distributing free tokens or coins to the community has been around for much longer than that. In fact, the first recorded airdrop took place in 2014, when the developers of the cryptocurrency Stellar (XLM) distributed 50 billion XLM to Bitcoin holders.

However, the idea of airdropping goes back even further. In the early days of the internet, companies would distribute free CDs or floppy disks to promote their products or services. The idea was that by giving away something for free, they could generate interest and attract new customers.

The same concept applies to airdrops in the cryptocurrency world. By giving away tokens or coins for free, companies can generate interest in their project and attract new users. But airdrops also serve another purpose: to distribute tokens or coins in a fair and equitable way.

In the early days of cryptocurrency, many projects would conduct initial coin offerings (ICOs) to raise funds for their development. However, ICOs were often criticized for being unfair, with early investors and insiders receiving a disproportionate amount of tokens or coins. Airdrops offer a way to distribute tokens or coins more fairly, as they are often distributed to a wide range of community members, rather than just investors.

Overall, the history of airdrops is closely tied to the evolution of cryptocurrency and the need to distribute tokens or coins in a fair and equitable way. As the crypto industry continues to grow and evolve, it's likely that we'll see even more innovative ways to distribute tokens and coins through airdrops.

A lesser-known fact about the history of airdrops is that they were originally used in the context of warfare. During World War II, Allied forces would use airdrops to deliver supplies and reinforcements to troops on the ground, especially in hard-to-reach or remote areas. This allowed them to quickly provide much-needed resources to their soldiers and help turn the tide of battle in their favor.

In the context of cryptocurrencies, the first airdrop is generally credited to the altcoin called Auroracoin, which was launched in 2014. The developers behind Auroracoin chose to distribute 50% of the total coins through an airdrop to citizens of Iceland, as a way to encourage adoption of the cryptocurrency in that country. This sparked the beginning of a trend, with many subsequent altcoins also using airdrops as a way to distribute their tokens or coins to potential users and investors.

The future of airdrops

The future of airdrops is promising and exciting. As the blockchain and cryptocurrency industry continue to evolve, airdrops are likely to remain a popular way for companies to distribute tokens and attract new users.

One trend that is expected to gain momentum is the use of airdrops as a marketing tool by established businesses outside the cryptocurrency industry. Companies in industries such as e-commerce, gaming, and social media could use airdrops to reward customers for their loyalty, incentivize new sign-ups, and even launch their own tokens.

Another trend that is emerging is the use of airdrops to promote social good. Projects are already using airdrops to raise awareness and funds for charitable causes. Going forward, we can expect to see more initiatives that leverage the power of airdrops to drive positive change in society.

The technology behind airdrops is also evolving, with new platforms and protocols being developed to make the process more efficient and secure. Decentralized finance (DeFi) projects are already experimenting with airdrops that use smart contracts to automate the distribution of tokens. These platforms eliminate the need for users to provide personal information, making the process more transparent and less vulnerable to fraud.

Overall, the future of airdrops looks bright. As the blockchain and cryptocurrency industry matures, airdrops are likely to become more sophisticated and mainstream, offering new opportunities for users to earn rewards and for companies to reach their target audience.

As the popularity of cryptocurrencies and blockchain technology continue to grow, the future of airdrops is bright. With more and more projects launching and competing for attention, airdrops may become even more prevalent as a way to gain exposure and generate interest in new projects.

One potential direction for the future of airdrops is increased use of smart contracts, which can automate the process and make it more efficient. This could also lead to a more targeted approach to airdrops, with projects able to more precisely identify and reward the users who are most likely to engage with their platform.

In addition, we may see a shift toward more creative and innovative types of airdrops. For example, some projects may offer airdrops to users who participate in their decentralized applications, or to those who complete specific tasks or challenges.

Another potential development is the integration of airdrops into other marketing strategies, such as social media campaigns or referral programs. This could help to expand the reach of airdrops and make them even more effective as a tool for generating interest and engagement.

Overall, the future of airdrops is exciting and full of possibilities. As the crypto and blockchain industries continue to evolve and mature, we can expect to see even more creative and effective uses of airdrops to drive adoption and engagement.

As the popularity of cryptocurrencies continues to rise, airdrops are likely to become an increasingly common method of distribution for new tokens and coins. However, as regulatory scrutiny on the cryptocurrency space grows, it's possible that airdrops may face stricter regulations in the future.

Some experts predict that the future of airdrops may move beyond simply distributing tokens to users for free. Instead, airdrops may become a more sophisticated marketing strategy that involves targeting specific user demographics and offering a range of incentives beyond just free tokens.

Furthermore, with the rise of decentralized finance (DeFi) platforms, airdrops may also be used to incentivize users to participate in governance and decision-making processes within these platforms. This could lead to a more democratic and decentralized future for the cryptocurrency space.

Overall, the future of airdrops is exciting and unpredictable. While some aspects may change as the industry evolves, the fundamental concept of distributing free tokens to users is likely to remain a popular and effective method of promoting new projects and building communities.

PART 2

Getting Started with Airdrops

CHAPTER **5**

GETTING STARTED WITH AIRDROPS

Getting started with airdrops can be intimidating for beginners, but it doesn't have to be. Here are some tips and tricks to help you get started with airdrops:

Do your research: Before participating in any airdrop, it's important to research the project and team behind it. Look for information on their website, social media, and other credible sources to ensure that the airdrop is legitimate.

Join crypto communities

Joining crypto communities such as Telegram groups, Discord channels, and Reddit communities can help you stay up to date with the latest airdrops. These communities often share information about upcoming airdrops, including how to participate and how much you can earn.

Joining crypto communities is a great way to stay up-to-date with the latest news and trends in the cryptocurrency world, and it can also provide opportunities for participating in airdrops. However, there are some lesser-known aspects to joining these communities that many people may not be aware of.

One of the benefits of joining a crypto community is the access it can provide to insider information. Many projects have official social media channels and forums where they share updates and interact with their followers. By following these channels, you may be among the first to learn about new projects and upcoming airdrops.

Another benefit of joining a crypto community is the opportunity to network with like-minded individuals. This can be especially valuable for those who are new to the cryptocurrency space and are looking to learn more from experienced traders and investors. By building relationships with others in the community, you may be able to gain valuable insights and tips for participating in airdrops.

It's also important to note that not all crypto communities are created equal. Some may be more active and informative than others, and some may be more focused on a specific type of cryptocurrency or investment strategy. It's a good idea to research different communities and find ones that align with your interests and goals.

In addition to official social media channels and forums, there are also a number of third-party websites and apps that aggregate information about upcoming airdrops and other crypto-related news. By using these resources, you can stay informed about new opportunities to participate in airdrops and potentially earn rewards.

Joining crypto communities is an essential step in participating in airdrops. These communities not only provide you with valuable information about upcoming airdrops but also help you connect with other like-minded individuals who share your interest in cryptocurrency.

When joining a crypto community, it's important to choose one that aligns with your interests and goals. For example, if you're interested in trading altcoins, you may want to join a community that focuses on altcoins and their development. On the other hand, if you're interested in investing in long-term projects, you may want to join a community that focuses on blockchain technology and its potential.

In addition to providing information about airdrops, crypto communities can also be valuable sources of knowledge and advice. Experienced members can help you navigate the often-complex world of cryptocurrency and provide guidance on investing and trading strategies.

There are many different types of crypto communities, including online forums, social media groups, and chat rooms. Some of the most popular include Bitcointalk, Reddit, Telegram, and Discord. Each of these communities has its own strengths and weaknesses, so it's important to explore different options and find one that best suits your needs.

It's also important to be an active and engaged member of these communities. By contributing to discussions, sharing your insights and knowledge, and helping others, you can build a reputation and establish yourself as a respected member of the community. This can open up new opportunities for airdrops and other crypto-related activities.

Get a cryptocurrency wallet: To participate in airdrops, you'll need a cryptocurrency wallet that supports the coins or tokens being distributed. Make sure to choose a reputable wallet that is compatible with the airdrop you want to participate in.

Stay organized: Keeping track of all the airdrops you've participated in can be challenging. Consider using a spreadsheet or a dedicated app to keep track of the airdrops you've joined, including the date, the amount of tokens or coins received, and any other relevant information.

Be patient: Airdrops can take some time to distribute, so be patient. Some airdrops can take weeks or even months to distribute the tokens or coins, so don't panic if you don't receive them right away.

Be cautious: While airdrops can be a great way to earn some free cryptocurrency, there are also many scams out there. Be cautious and never share your private keys or seed phrases with anyone.

By following these tips, you can get started with airdrops and potentially earn some free cryptocurrency along the way.

Set up a dedicated email address: Since airdrops often require you to share your email address, it's a good idea to create a separate email account to avoid cluttering your personal or work email inbox.

Follow official channels: To stay up to date on the latest airdrop opportunities, it's important to follow official social media channels for the projects you're interested in. This can include Twitter, Telegram, and Discord.

Be cautious of scams: Unfortunately, there are many scams in the airdrop space. Be wary of any airdrops that require you to send cryptocurrency or provide sensitive personal information. Always do your due diligence and research the project and team behind the airdrop.

Use a secure wallet: When participating in airdrops, it's important to use a secure wallet to receive your tokens. Popular options include MyEtherWallet and MetaMask. Avoid using exchanges as your receiving wallet, as some airdrops require you to hold tokens in a non-exchange wallet to be eligible.

Keep track of your airdrops: It's a good idea to keep a spreadsheet or document to track your airdrops and their value. This can help you stay organized and ensure that you don't miss out on claiming your tokens.

Be patient: Airdrops can take time to distribute, so be patient and don't panic if you don't receive your tokens right away. It's also worth noting that some airdrops may have restrictions on when you can sell or trade the tokens, so make sure to read the terms and conditions carefully.

By following these tips and doing your research, you can get started with airdrops and potentially earn some free cryptocurrency.

How to find airdrops

To find airdrops, you can use a variety of methods. Here are some tips to help you find them:

Follow social media accounts of crypto projects and exchanges: Many companies will announce their airdrops on their social media accounts, so following them is a good way to stay up-to-date.

Join crypto communities: Participating in crypto communities, such as Telegram groups or Discord channels, can also be a good way to find airdrops. Many projects will announce their airdrops in these communities.

Use airdrop tracking websites: There are a number of websites that track airdrops and provide information on when they are happening and how to participate. Some popular options include AirdropAlert, Airdrop King, and Airdrop Bob.

Check crypto news websites: Many crypto news websites, such as CoinDesk and CryptoSlate, will also announce upcoming airdrops and provide information on how to participate.

Join bounty programs: Some airdrops are tied to bounty programs, which offer rewards for completing specific tasks, such as promoting the project on social media or writing articles about it. By participating in these bounty programs, you may also be eligible for airdrops.

It's important to note that not all airdrops are legitimate, so be sure to do your research before participating. Scammers often create fake airdrops to steal users' personal information or funds, so be cautious and only participate in airdrops from reputable projects.

Here are some additional tips on how to find airdrops:

Follow social media accounts: Many companies and projects promoting airdrops will announce them on their social media accounts. Make sure to follow them and keep an eye out for any updates.

Check crypto news websites: Cryptocurrency news websites often feature articles about upcoming airdrops. Check regularly to stay up to date on the latest airdrop news.

Join Telegram groups: Many crypto projects have Telegram groups where they announce airdrops and other promotions. Joining these groups can give you early access to airdrop information and potentially increase your chances of getting in.

Use airdrop aggregator websites: Airdrop aggregator websites like Airdrop Alert and Airdrops.io compile lists of current and upcoming airdrops. These sites can save you time and help you find airdrops you may not have heard of otherwise.

Participate in referral programs: Some airdrops have referral programs that reward you for getting other people to sign up. If you know other people interested in airdrops, this can be a good way to earn additional tokens.

Remember to always do your own research before participating in an airdrop to ensure it is legitimate and worth your time.

How to register for airdrops

To register for airdrops, follow these steps:

Set up a wallet: Before registering for an airdrop, you need to have a compatible wallet for the specific token or coin. Make sure you set up a secure wallet and keep your private keys safe.

Join the project's community: To participate in an airdrop, you need to be part of the project's community. Join their social media groups like Telegram, Discord, Reddit, Twitter, or follow their official channels.

Complete KYC: Some airdrops require Know Your Customer (KYC) verification. KYC is a process of verifying your identity, such as your name, address, and date of birth. To complete the KYC process, you need to provide personal identification documents like passport, driver's license, or national ID.

Fill out the airdrop form: Once you've joined the community and completed the KYC process, you can fill out the airdrop form. The form will typically ask for your email address, social media handles, wallet address, and other details required for the airdrop.

Follow instructions: After filling out the form, follow the instructions provided by the project. Some airdrops may require you to perform specific actions like following their social media pages, referring friends, or completing tasks to receive the tokens.

Wait for the distribution: After you've completed all the steps, wait for the distribution of tokens. It can take several weeks or even months for the tokens to be distributed, so be patient.

It's important to note that not all airdrops are worth participating in, and some may be scams. Do your due diligence before participating in any airdrops and never give out your private keys or personal information to anyone claiming to be associated with the project.

Use a dedicated email address: Since you'll likely be signing up for a lot of different airdrops, it's a good idea to use a dedicated email address for these registrations. This will help you keep track of all the emails and notifications you receive.

Enable two-factor authentication: Many airdrop registration forms will ask you to provide your email address and phone number. To ensure your account is secure, it's recommended to enable two-factor authentication (2FA) on your email and phone accounts.

Read the terms and conditions: It's important to read the terms and conditions of each airdrop you sign up for. Some airdrops may have specific requirements or restrictions, such as only being available to residents of certain countries.

Provide accurate information: When registering for an airdrop, be sure to provide accurate information. This includes your name, email address, and any other required information. Providing false or misleading information could disqualify you from receiving the airdrop.

Check your eligibility: Before registering for an airdrop, check to see if you are eligible to participate. Some airdrops may have specific requirements, such as holding a certain amount of a particular cryptocurrency.

Use a VPN: Some airdrops may only be available in certain countries. If you're not located in one of those countries, you may still be able to participate by using a virtual private network (VPN) to access the registration form.

Don't pay to participate: Legitimate airdrops are free to participate in. If a registration form asks you to pay a fee to participate, it's likely a scam.

By following these tips, you can increase your chances of successfully registering for airdrops and receiving free cryptocurrency tokens.

Wallets and exchanges for airdrops

Wallets and exchanges play a crucial role in participating in airdrops, as this is where you receive and store the tokens you earn. Here are some things many people may not know about wallets and exchanges for airdrops:

Compatibility: Before participating in an airdrop, you should ensure that your wallet or exchange is compatible with the token you will receive. Some tokens are only compatible with certain wallets or exchanges, so it's important to do your research beforehand.

Security: As with any cryptocurrency transaction, security should be a top priority. Ensure that the wallet or exchange you choose has robust security measures in place, such as two-factor authentication and cold storage options.

KYC and AML: Some exchanges and wallets may require you to complete Know Your Customer (KYC) and Anti-Money Laundering (AML) checks before participating in an airdrop. This is to ensure compliance with regulations and prevent fraudulent activities.

Reputation: When choosing a wallet or exchange, it's important to consider their reputation in the cryptocurrency community. Look for reviews, user experiences, and any past security incidents to make an informed decision.

Fees: Some wallets and exchanges may charge fees for receiving or withdrawing tokens from an airdrop. Be sure to check for any applicable fees before participating.

Claiming tokens

Some airdrops may require you to claim the tokens manually, while others may automatically send the tokens to your wallet or exchange. Make sure you understand the process for claiming tokens before participating in the airdrop.

An airdrop is a marketing strategy used by blockchain and cryptocurrency projects to distribute their tokens or coins for free to a large number of people. The purpose of an airdrop is to generate buzz, attract new users, and create a broad community around a project.

When a project conducts an airdrop, they usually distribute the tokens or coins to participants who meet specific criteria. For example, participants might need to hold a certain amount of a specific cryptocurrency, complete a survey, or follow the project on social media.

Once the airdrop is over, participants need to claim their tokens or coins. However, many people are not aware of some important things related to claiming airdropped tokens. Here are a few things that many people might not know about claiming airdrop tokens:

Time Limitations: Some airdrops have a time limit for claiming the tokens. Participants need to claim their tokens before the deadline, or they will forfeit the tokens.

Claiming Process: The claiming process can be different for each airdrop. Participants need to follow the specific instructions given by the project to claim their tokens. This could involve creating a new wallet, adding a specific smart contract, or completing a KYC process.

Gas Fees: When claiming airdropped tokens, participants may need to pay gas fees to complete the transaction. Gas fees are used to pay miners to process the transaction on the blockchain. Participants should be aware of the gas fees involved and ensure they have enough funds to pay them.

Taxation: Airdrops may be taxable events depending on the country of residence and the value of the tokens received. Participants should consult with a tax professional to understand their tax obligations related to airdropped tokens.

Scams: There are many scams related to airdrops, where fraudsters pose as legitimate projects and ask participants to send their private keys or pay a fee to claim the tokens. Participants should be cautious and verify the legitimacy of the project before claiming any airdropped tokens.

Claiming airdropped tokens can be a great way to get involved in a new blockchain or cryptocurrency project. However, participants should be aware of the specific instructions, time limitations, gas fees, tax implications, and scams related to claiming airdropped tokens.

Here are some additional things that you may not know about claiming airdropped tokens:

Wallet Compatibility: Some airdrops are only compatible with certain types of wallets. For example, an airdrop may require participants to use a wallet that supports the ERC-20 standard if the token is built on the Ethereum blockchain. Participants should check the airdrop instructions to ensure that their wallet is compatible with the airdropped token.

Token Value: The value of airdropped tokens can vary widely. While some tokens may be worth a significant amount of money, others may be virtually worthless. Participants should research the project and the token before claiming it to determine its potential value.

Distribution Timeframe: Airdropped tokens may not be distributed immediately after the airdrop is over. It may take some time for the project to process and distribute the tokens. Participants should be patient and check the project's website or social media channels for updates on token distribution.

Whitelisting: Some airdrops require participants to whitelist their wallet addresses before the airdrop begins. This involves registering the wallet address with the project and providing personal information such as name and email address. Participants should be cautious when providing personal information and ensure that they are dealing with a legitimate project.

Holding Requirements: Some airdrops require participants to hold the airdropped tokens for a certain period before they can sell or trade them. Participants should be aware of any holding requirements before claiming the airdropped tokens.

Claiming airdropped tokens can be a fun and exciting way to get involved in a new blockchain or cryptocurrency project. However, participants should take the time to understand the specific instructions, wallet compatibility, token value, distribution timeframe, whitelisting requirements, and holding requirements related to claiming airdropped tokens. By doing so, participants can ensure that they are claiming legitimate tokens and avoid falling victim to scams or other pitfalls associated with airdrops.

Overall, choosing the right wallet or exchange for participating in airdrops can have a significant impact on your experience and the security of your tokens. Be sure to research and choose wisely.

When it comes to participating in airdrops, choosing the right wallet or exchange is essential. Here are a few things that many people may not know about wallets and exchanges for airdrops:

Not all wallets and exchanges support airdrops: Before registering for an airdrop, it's important to check if your chosen wallet or exchange supports that particular token. Some wallets or exchanges may not support certain tokens, which means you won't be able to receive the airdrop.

Use a wallet with private keys: When participating in an airdrop, it's important to use a wallet that gives you control of your private keys. This means you have complete control over your tokens and can access them even if the wallet or exchange goes down.

Check for compatibility: Some airdrops may only be compatible with certain wallets or exchanges. Before registering for an airdrop, make sure you check if your wallet or exchange is compatible with the airdrop token.

Consider security: When using wallets or exchanges, security is always a top priority. Look for wallets and exchanges with a good reputation for security and consider using hardware wallets or multi-signature wallets for extra security.

Be aware of fees: Some wallets or exchanges may charge fees for receiving airdrops. Make sure you read the terms and conditions carefully to avoid any surprises. Additionally, some airdrops may require you to hold a certain amount of tokens in your wallet or exchange, which may also come with fees.

Overall, it's important to do your research before choosing a wallet or exchange for airdrops. Make sure you choose a reputable provider that supports the tokens you're interested in, and consider security and fees when making your decision.

Airdrop eligibility requirements

Airdrops can come with various eligibility requirements, which are often set by the project or company offering the airdrop. Here are some common eligibility requirements that many people may not be aware of:

Geographic restrictions: Some airdrops may only be available to residents of certain countries. This is often due to regulatory or legal considerations, or simply because the company is targeting a specific market.

KYC/AML requirements: Know Your Customer (KYC) and Anti-Money Laundering (AML) requirements are becoming increasingly common in the cryptocurrency space. Some airdrops may require participants to complete a KYC/AML verification process in order to be eligible.

Holding requirements: Some airdrops require participants to hold a certain amount of a specific cryptocurrency in their wallet in order to be eligible. This is often referred to as a "staking requirement".

Social media engagement: Many airdrops require participants to engage with the project or company on social media platforms, such as Twitter or Telegram. This may include following the project, retweeting or sharing posts, or participating in community discussions.

Referral requirements: Some airdrops offer additional rewards for referring new participants to the airdrop. In these cases, participants may be required to share a unique referral link or code with their friends and followers.

It's important to carefully review the eligibility requirements for any airdrop you are interested in participating in, as failing to meet the requirements may result in disqualification from the airdrop.

KYC/AML Compliance: Some airdrops require participants to complete KYC/AML (Know Your Customer/Anti-Money Laundering) verification procedures in order to be eligible to receive the airdrop. This is usually done to comply with regulatory requirements or to prevent fraud.

Geographic Restrictions: Some airdrops may be limited to certain geographic regions due to legal or regulatory reasons, or the preference of the project organizers.

Holding Requirements: Some airdrops may require participants to hold a certain amount of a specific cryptocurrency in order to be eligible for the airdrop. This is often done to incentivize long-term holding of the cryptocurrency.

Participation Requirements: Some airdrops may require participants to complete certain tasks, such as following the project on social media, posting about the project on social media, or participating in a survey or quiz.

Wallet Requirements: Some airdrops may require participants to hold their cryptocurrency in a specific type of wallet, such as a hardware wallet, a specific software wallet, or an exchange wallet.

Token Swap Requirements: Some airdrops may require participants to swap their existing cryptocurrency for a new token in order to be eligible for the airdrop. This is often done to incentivize participants to migrate to a new blockchain or platform.

It's important to carefully read the eligibility requirements for each airdrop you are interested in participating in, as they can vary widely and may impact your eligibility to receive the airdrop tokens.

How to maximize your chances of getting airdropped tokens

Getting airdropped tokens is not always a guaranteed process, but there are some tips that can help maximize your chances of receiving tokens:

Join multiple platforms: Joining multiple platforms such as Twitter, Telegram, Reddit, and Discord can help increase your chances of finding and participating in airdrops. Many projects use different platforms to promote their airdrops, so by joining all relevant platforms, you'll be able to stay on top of the latest opportunities.

Verify your identity: Many airdrops require you to verify your identity through KYC (Know Your Customer) procedures. Completing the KYC process is essential to ensuring that you meet the eligibility requirements of the airdrop and can receive your tokens.

Participate actively: Many airdrops require active participation, such as retweeting, commenting, or sharing the project's content. Participating actively can help increase your chances of receiving tokens.

Be aware of the deadline: Most airdrops have a deadline, so it's important to make sure you participate before the deadline. Some airdrops may require you to hold the tokens for a certain period of time, so make sure you understand the requirements before participating.

Be cautious: Be cautious when participating in airdrops, especially if they require you to provide personal information or access to your wallet. Only participate in airdrops from reputable projects and be wary of scams.

Use multiple wallets: It is often recommended to use multiple wallets when participating in airdrops. This is because some projects may not be compatible with certain wallets, and using multiple wallets can help increase your chances of receiving tokens.

Stay up-to-date: Keep up-to-date with the latest news and updates from the projects you participate in. Some airdrops may require additional actions or steps to receive the tokens, and staying up-to-date can help ensure that you don't miss any important information.

Here are some additional tips to help you maximize your chances of getting airdropped tokens:

Stay active in the crypto community: Many airdrops require participants to be active in the crypto community, such as by following specific social media accounts or joining Telegram groups. Make sure you are actively engaging with these communities to increase your chances of being selected for an airdrop.

Join multiple airdrop platforms: There are several websites and platforms that list ongoing and upcoming airdrops. Joining multiple platforms increases your chances of discovering new airdrops that you might not find elsewhere.

Keep your social media profiles updated: Airdrops often require participants to follow specific social media accounts or share content on their own social media profiles. Make sure your profiles are up-to-date and active to improve your chances of being selected.

Participate in referral programs: Many airdrops offer referral bonuses, where you receive additional tokens for every person you refer to the airdrop. If you have a strong network in the crypto community, this can be a great way to earn more tokens.

Follow instructions carefully: Airdrops often have specific instructions that participants must follow in order to be eligible for the tokens. Make sure you read and follow these instructions carefully to avoid disqualification.

Be patient: Airdrops can take time to distribute tokens, so be patient and wait for the airdrop to complete before assuming you were not selected.

By following these tips, you can increase your chances of receiving airdropped tokens and maximizing your rewards in the crypto world.

PART 3

Participating in Airdrops

Chapter 6
Participating in Airdrops

Participating in airdrops is a great way to earn free tokens or cryptocurrencies, but there are some things to keep in mind to maximize your chances of success. Here are some tips:

Be mindful of scams: Unfortunately, there are many fake airdrops out there, so it's important to do your due diligence and only participate in airdrops from reputable sources. Never give out your private keys or seed phrases, and always double-check the official website or social media channels of the project before participating.

Join multiple airdrops: To increase your chances of receiving tokens, consider joining multiple airdrops. There are many resources online that list ongoing and upcoming airdrops, so do your research and sign up for those that interest you.

Follow the rules: Each airdrop will have its own set of rules and requirements, so make sure you understand and follow them carefully. This might include completing certain tasks, holding a certain amount of tokens, or verifying your identity.

Be patient: Airdrops often have limited supplies, so it may take some time before you receive your tokens. Be patient and keep an eye on the project's social media channels for updates.

Use a dedicated email address: To avoid cluttering your main inbox, consider using a dedicated email address for airdrop sign-ups. This will make it easier to keep track of which projects you have signed up for and avoid missing important updates.

Consider the long-term potential: While it's tempting to participate in every airdrop you come across, it's important to do your research and consider the long-term potential of the project. Don't just join an airdrop because it offers a quick payout - make sure the project has a solid team, clear vision, and potential for growth.

Manage your expectations: Remember that airdrops are not a guaranteed source of income, and the value of the tokens you receive may fluctuate. Manage your expectations and don't invest more than you can afford to lose.

Overall, participating in airdrops can be a fun and potentially rewarding way to get involved in the world of cryptocurrencies. With some research, patience, and a bit of luck, you can maximize your chances of success and earn some free tokens along the way.

Here are some additional things to consider when participating in airdrops:

Be cautious of scams: Airdrops can be a prime target for scammers looking to steal personal information or cryptocurrency. Be sure to verify the legitimacy of the airdrop and the company or project offering it before participating.

Pay attention to the rules: Each airdrop will have its own set of rules and requirements for participation. Be sure to read and understand these rules carefully to ensure you are eligible and follow all necessary steps to receive the airdropped tokens.

Keep track of your airdrops: As you participate in various airdrops, it can be helpful to keep track of which tokens you've received, their value, and any relevant dates or deadlines. This can help you stay organized and make informed decisions about your cryptocurrency holdings.

Consider the long-term value: While airdrops can be a fun way to receive free tokens, it's important to consider the long-term value of these tokens before investing in them. Research the project and its team, technology, and market potential to determine if it's worth holding onto the tokens or selling them.

Stay up-to-date on the latest airdrops: Airdrops can be a fast-moving market, with new opportunities popping up regularly. Stay up-to-date on the latest airdrops by following relevant cryptocurrency news sources and social media accounts. Additionally, consider joining airdrop-specific communities or forums to stay informed and potentially discover new opportunities.

What to do after you receive an airdrop

Congratulations, you've received an airdrop! Now what? Here are some steps you can take to make the most out of your airdropped tokens:

Research the project: Before doing anything else, it's important to understand what the project is all about. Read the whitepaper, check out the website, and follow the project on social media. This will help you make informed decisions about what to do with your tokens.

Evaluate the token: Once you've done your research, evaluate the token itself. Look at factors such as its market capitalization, trading volume, and price history. This will give you a sense of the token's potential value and whether it's worth holding or selling.

Decide what to do with the tokens: Depending on your goals and risk tolerance, you may decide to hold onto the tokens, sell them immediately, or trade them for other cryptocurrencies. Just remember that there may be tax implications for any gains or losses you realize.

Secure your tokens: Whether you plan to hold onto your tokens or sell them, it's important to keep them secure. Transfer them to a secure wallet or exchange and enable two-factor authentication (2FA) to protect your account.

Keep an eye on the project: Even if you decide to sell your tokens, it's a good idea to keep an eye on the project's progress. You never know when a project may take off and increase in value, and staying informed can help you make better decisions in the future.

Consider participating in future airdrops: If you've received an airdrop from a project you believe in, consider participating in future airdrops or even becoming an active member of the community. This can help you earn more tokens and stay up-to-date on the project's progress.

Remember, airdrops can be a great way to get involved in the cryptocurrency space and potentially earn some free tokens. By doing your research and taking steps to secure your tokens, you can make the most out of any airdrop you receive.

There are several things you can do after receiving an airdrop to make the most of your free tokens. Here are some tips:

Store your tokens securely: It's important to store your tokens in a secure wallet to protect them from theft or loss. Consider using a hardware wallet or a trusted software wallet that supports the specific tokens you received.

Monitor the value of your tokens: Keep an eye on the value of your tokens to determine whether to hold, sell or trade them. Some tokens may appreciate in value over time, while others may lose value. Do your own research and consult with financial advisors if necessary.

Participate in the project: Learn more about the project behind the tokens you received and consider participating in the community. This could involve joining the project's social media channels, attending events or meetups, or contributing to the project's development.

Sell or trade your tokens: If you don't believe in the project or don't want to hold onto the tokens, you can consider selling or trading them. There are various cryptocurrency exchanges where you can buy and sell tokens, but be sure to do your own research and choose a reputable exchange.

Pay attention to tax implications: Depending on where you live, you may be required to pay taxes on the value of the tokens you received. Consult with a tax professional to ensure that you comply with any relevant tax laws.

Overall, receiving an airdrop can be an exciting opportunity to receive free tokens and potentially participate in a new project. By following these tips, you can make the most of your airdrop and potentially benefit from its value.

How to claim airdropped tokens

To claim airdropped tokens, the process typically involves a few steps, and the exact process can vary depending on the project and the distribution method. Here are some general steps to follow:

Check your eligibility: Before claiming any airdropped tokens, make sure you are eligible for them. This includes checking the requirements such as holding a specific cryptocurrency, having a certain wallet, or completing specific tasks.

Verify your identity: Some airdrops may require you to complete a KYC (Know Your Customer) process before you can claim your tokens. This is usually done to comply with regulations and prevent fraud.

Access your wallet: If you are using a hardware wallet or a wallet that doesn't support the airdropped token, you may need to transfer your tokens to a compatible wallet to claim them.

Claim the tokens: Depending on the distribution method, you may need to complete specific steps to claim your tokens. This can include submitting a form, signing a message with your private key, or interacting with a smart contract.

Monitor your tokens: Once you've claimed your tokens, keep an eye on their value and any potential developments related to the project. Some airdrops may require you to hold the tokens for a specific period or meet other requirements to keep them.

It's essential to stay aware of scams when claiming airdropped tokens. Be sure to verify the legitimacy of the airdrop before submitting any personal information or sending tokens to an address.

Here are additional tips for claiming airdropped tokens:

Check if you are eligible: Before claiming any airdropped tokens, make sure that you are eligible. Read the terms and conditions of the airdrop carefully to determine if there are any specific eligibility requirements. For example, some airdrops may only be available to residents of certain countries or holders of a particular cryptocurrency.

Follow the instructions: Each airdrop may have different instructions for claiming the tokens. Be sure to read the instructions carefully and follow them precisely. This may involve creating an account on a specific platform, verifying your identity, or completing a specific task.

Keep your private key safe: When claiming your airdropped tokens, you will need to access your wallet or exchange account. Make sure you keep your private key safe and never share it with anyone. If your private key falls into the wrong hands, your tokens may be stolen.

Be patient: Some airdrops may take several days or even weeks to be credited to your account. Be patient and wait for the tokens to arrive. However, if you have not received the tokens within a reasonable timeframe, you may want to contact the airdrop team for assistance.

Consider taxes: Depending on your jurisdiction, receiving airdropped tokens may trigger a tax event. Make sure you consult a tax professional to understand the tax implications of receiving and holding airdropped tokens.

Don't fall for scams: Unfortunately, there are many scams in the crypto space, and airdrops are no exception. Be wary of any airdrops that require you to send cryptocurrency or personal information in exchange for tokens. Legitimate airdrops will never ask for this information.

How to store airdropped tokens

When it comes to storing airdropped tokens, it's essential to keep them safe and secure. Here are some tips on how to store your airdropped tokens:

Hardware Wallets: Consider using a hardware wallet such as Ledger or Trezor to store your airdropped tokens. Hardware wallets are the most secure way to store your tokens since they store your private keys offline, making them less susceptible to hacking attempts.

Software Wallets

A software wallet is a digital wallet that stores cryptocurrency on software installed on a computer or mobile device. Here are some things that many people may not know about software wallets:

Security: Software wallets are not as secure as hardware wallets because they are vulnerable to malware and hacking. It is important to take necessary precautions such as keeping your operating system and antivirus software up to date, and not storing large amounts of cryptocurrency on your software wallet.

Types of software wallets: There are several types of software wallets, including desktop wallets, mobile wallets, and web wallets. Desktop wallets are installed on a computer, mobile wallets are installed on a smartphone, and web wallets are accessed through a web browser.

Private keys: Software wallets store the private keys that give you access to your cryptocurrency. It is important to back up your private keys and store them in a safe place in case you lose access to your wallet.

Fees: Some software wallets may charge transaction fees for sending cryptocurrency. It is important to research the fees associated with different software wallets to find one that fits your needs.

User experience: The user experience of software wallets can vary widely depending on the wallet. Some wallets may have more user-friendly interfaces and features than others, so it is important to try out different wallets to find one that works best for you.

Here's more information on software wallets:

Software wallets, also known as hot wallets, are digital wallets that store your cryptocurrency on your computer or mobile device. They are called "hot" wallets because they are connected to the internet and are always online. This makes them convenient and easy to use, but also makes them more vulnerable to hacking and theft than other types of wallets.

One of the advantages of software wallets is that they are often free to download and use. They are also user-friendly and can be accessed through a desktop or mobile app. Some of the popular software wallets include:

Exodus: This is a popular desktop wallet that supports multiple cryptocurrencies, including Bitcoin, Ethereum, and Litecoin. It has a user-friendly interface and allows users to exchange cryptocurrencies within the wallet.

MyEtherWallet: This is a free, open-source wallet that is designed specifically for Ethereum and ERC-20 tokens. It is an online wallet that can be accessed through a web browser and is known for its security features.

Atomic Wallet: This is a desktop and mobile wallet that supports more than 500 cryptocurrencies. It allows users to buy and sell cryptocurrencies within the wallet and has a built-in exchange.

Trust Wallet: This is a mobile wallet that is available for both Android and iOS devices. It is known for its security features and supports a wide range of cryptocurrencies.

While software wallets are convenient, it's important to remember that they are not as secure as hardware wallets. They are vulnerable to hacking, malware, and other security threats. Therefore, it's important to follow best practices for keeping your software wallet secure, such as using two-factor authentication and keeping your private keys safe.

If you prefer to use a software wallet, choose one that is reputable and secure, such as MyEtherWallet or MetaMask. These wallets allow you to store your private keys on your device, but it's essential to ensure that your device is free from malware and viruses.

Exchange Wallets: While storing your tokens on an exchange wallet is convenient, it's not the most secure option. If you do choose to store your tokens on an exchange, consider using an exchange with a strong reputation for security, and enable two-factor authentication.

Back up your wallet: Regardless of which wallet you choose, it's essential to back up your wallet in case of device loss or failure. Keep a copy of your private keys or seed phrase in a secure location, such as a safe or a safety deposit box.

Check for token support: Not all wallets support every token. Before sending your airdropped tokens to a wallet, check to ensure that the wallet supports the token. Otherwise, you risk losing your tokens.

Keep track of your tokens: Keep a record of your airdropped tokens, including the date received and the token's value at that time. This information will help you keep track of your portfolio's performance and provide a clear record for tax purposes.

Storing airdropped tokens requires careful consideration of security and compatibility. Choose a wallet that suits your needs and enables you to maintain control over your tokens.

When it comes to storing airdropped tokens, it is essential to understand the different options available and to choose the one that best fits your needs.

The first option is to store the tokens on the same wallet or exchange where you received them. This can be a convenient option, as the tokens are already in that wallet or exchange, and you can easily access and manage them. However, it is important to remember that exchanges are not the safest place to store cryptocurrencies. If the exchange is hacked or goes bankrupt, your tokens could be lost. Therefore, it is recommended to transfer the tokens to a personal wallet as soon as possible.

The second option is to use a hardware wallet, which is a physical device that stores your cryptocurrencies offline. Hardware wallets provide the highest level of security and are an excellent option for those who hold a significant amount of cryptocurrencies. Some popular hardware wallet brands include Ledger, Trezor, and KeepKey.

Another option is to use a software wallet, which is a digital wallet that stores your cryptocurrencies on your computer or mobile device. There are many software wallets available, such as MyEtherWallet, Exodus, and Trust Wallet. It is essential to choose a reputable wallet and to take proper security measures, such as setting up two-factor authentication and keeping your private keys safe.

Overall, storing airdropped tokens requires careful consideration of your security needs and the available options. It is essential to choose a secure storage method and to take appropriate precautions to protect your tokens.

How to sell or trade airdropped tokens

Once you have received your airdropped tokens, you may want to sell or trade them for other cryptocurrencies or fiat currencies. Here are some steps to follow:

Check the value: Before you sell or trade your airdropped tokens, it is important to check their current value in the market. You can use cryptocurrency price tracking websites or exchanges to get an idea of the current value.

Choose an exchange: You will need to choose an exchange that supports the trading or selling of your airdropped tokens. Some exchanges may not support all types of tokens, so it is important to check the exchange's listings.

Create an account: Once you have chosen an exchange, you will need to create an account. This will involve providing some personal information and creating a login and password.

Transfer tokens: To sell or trade your airdropped tokens, you will need to transfer them to your exchange wallet. This will involve creating a new wallet address for the specific token and transferring the tokens from your software or hardware wallet to the exchange wallet.

Sell or trade: Once your tokens are in the exchange wallet, you can sell or trade them for other cryptocurrencies or fiat currencies. Some exchanges allow you to place market or limit orders, which allow you to set the price you want to sell or trade at.

Withdraw: Finally, once you have sold or traded your tokens, you can withdraw the funds to your bank account or cryptocurrency wallet.

It is important to note that selling or trading cryptocurrencies can be risky, and the market value of the tokens can be volatile. It is important to do your research and consider the risks before making any trades. Additionally, depending on the exchange and the country you are in, there may be taxes and fees associated with selling or trading cryptocurrencies.

Here are some additional details on selling or trading airdropped tokens:

Choose a cryptocurrency exchange: To sell or trade airdropped tokens, you'll need to find a cryptocurrency exchange that supports the token. Some popular exchanges include Binance, Coinbase, and Kraken.

Create an account: Once you've selected an exchange, you'll need to create an account and complete any required verification steps.

Transfer your tokens: Next, you'll need to transfer your airdropped tokens from your wallet to your exchange account. You'll typically do this by sending the tokens to a deposit address provided by the exchange.

Sell or trade your tokens: Once your tokens have arrived in your exchange account, you can sell them for another cryptocurrency or fiat currency, or trade them for another cryptocurrency. The exact process will depend on the exchange you're using, but most exchanges have a simple interface that allows you to place buy and sell orders.

Withdraw your funds: After you've sold or traded your tokens, you can withdraw your funds to your bank account or to another cryptocurrency wallet. Again, the exact process will depend on the exchange you're using, but most exchanges have a simple withdrawal process.

It's important to note that selling or trading airdropped tokens can be risky, as the value of the token may be volatile and subject to sudden price swings. It's important to do your research and understand the risks before making any trades or selling your tokens. Additionally, you may be subject to taxes on any gains you make from selling or trading airdropped tokens, so it's important to keep accurate records of your transactions.

Tax considerations for airdrops

As with any cryptocurrency transaction, airdrops may have tax implications depending on your country's tax laws. Many people may not be aware of the tax considerations for airdrops, but it's important to be informed to avoid any potential legal issues.

In general, receiving airdropped tokens is considered a taxable event. The value of the tokens at the time of receipt is considered income, and you will need to report it on your tax return. This means that you may owe taxes on the value of the tokens, even if you don't sell them.

The tax treatment of airdrops can vary depending on your country's tax laws, and it's important to consult a tax professional for advice. Some countries may treat airdrops as capital gains, while others may consider them as ordinary income.

One important consideration is the cost basis of the airdropped tokens. Since airdropped tokens are typically received for free, it can be difficult to determine their cost basis. One method is to use the fair market value of the tokens at the time of receipt as the cost basis.

It's important to keep detailed records of all your airdrops, including the date of receipt, the fair market value at the time of receipt, and any subsequent transactions involving the tokens. This will help you accurately calculate your tax liability.

In summary, while airdrops can be a great way to receive free tokens, it's important to be aware of the tax implications and consult a tax professional for advice. Keeping detailed records can help you accurately report your airdrop income and avoid any potential legal issues.

When it comes to tax considerations for airdrops, it's important to note that receiving an airdrop does not necessarily mean that you owe taxes. However, there are a few situations where taxes may be owed:

Income tax: If you receive an airdrop and sell it for a profit, that profit may be subject to income tax. The tax rate will depend on your income bracket and the holding period of the tokens. In the United States, the IRS treats cryptocurrencies like property for tax purposes, so the tax treatment of airdrops will depend on how the IRS classifies the specific tokens.

Gift tax: If you receive an airdrop and then give it away, that may be subject to gift tax. The amount of the gift tax will depend on the value of the tokens and the applicable tax laws in your jurisdiction.

Estate tax: If you receive an airdrop and then pass away, the value of the tokens may be subject to estate tax.

It's important to consult with a tax professional to understand the tax implications of airdrops in your specific situation, especially if you plan on selling or trading the tokens. Additionally, it's a good practice to keep accurate records of all cryptocurrency transactions, including airdrops, in order to properly report them on your tax return.

It is important to note that tax laws regarding cryptocurrencies and airdrops vary by country and can be complex. Therefore, it is recommended to consult a tax professional or accountant to ensure compliance with tax regulations.

In general, in the United States, airdrops are considered taxable events and are subject to taxes on the fair market value of the tokens received at the time of receipt. This means that if you receive airdropped tokens worth $1,000, you may owe taxes on that amount, even if you do not sell or trade the tokens.

The tax rate will depend on several factors, including the holding period and the taxpayer's income tax bracket. In some cases, airdropped tokens may be considered ordinary income and subject to higher tax rates.

Additionally, if the airdrop is received as a result of a hard fork, it may be treated as a capital gain or loss, depending on how long the tokens are held before being sold or exchanged.

It is important to keep accurate records of all airdrop transactions and consult with a tax professional to ensure proper tax reporting. Failing to properly report airdrop transactions could result in penalties or fines from the tax authority.

PART 4
Airdrop Platforms

Chapter 7
Airdrop Platforms

Airdrop platforms are websites or online platforms that specialize in listing upcoming and ongoing airdrops, allowing users to easily discover, participate in, and track airdrops. Here are some things that many people may not know about airdrop platforms:

There are many airdrop platforms out there: While some of the most popular airdrop platforms include Airdrop Alert, Airdrops.io, and Airdrop King, there are many other platforms available that can help you discover airdrops that may not be listed on these larger platforms.

Some airdrop platforms are selective: Some airdrop platforms require users to complete various tasks, such as joining a Telegram group, following social media accounts, or sharing posts, before they can participate in airdrops. This is done to ensure that only serious users are participating in the airdrops, which can increase the value of the airdropped tokens.

Some airdrop platforms charge fees: While many airdrop platforms are free to use, some may charge fees for premium services or access to exclusive airdrops. It is important to research airdrop platforms and their fee structures before deciding which platform to use.

Some airdrop platforms have referral programs: Some airdrop platforms offer users the opportunity to earn additional tokens by referring new users to the platform. These referral programs can be a great way to earn even more tokens from airdrops.

Airdrop platforms can be a valuable resource for staying up-to-date on airdrops: By regularly checking airdrop platforms, users can stay informed about upcoming and ongoing airdrops, which can help them discover new opportunities to earn free tokens.

It is important to note that while airdrop platforms can be a useful tool for discovering and participating in airdrops, users should still exercise caution and do their own research before participating in any airdrop.

Airdrop platforms are websites or applications that provide information on upcoming airdrops, allowing users to participate and claim free tokens. These platforms usually collect information from various sources to compile a list of airdrops, making it easier for users to discover and participate in them.

One thing many people may not know is that there are several types of airdrop platforms available, each with its own unique features and benefits. Some platforms offer a curated list of airdrops, while others may offer tools and resources to help users manage their airdropped tokens. Additionally, some platforms may require users to complete certain tasks or meet certain criteria to access airdrops, while others may provide a more streamlined process for claiming tokens.

Another important thing to note is that not all airdrop platforms are legitimate or trustworthy. Some platforms may be scams or may not provide accurate information, so it's important to do your research and choose a reputable platform before participating in any airdrops. Look for platforms with positive reviews and a history of providing accurate information, and always be cautious of platforms that require you to provide personal or sensitive information.

Some popular airdrop platforms include Airdrop Alert, AirdropBob, Airdrop King, and Crypto Airdrops. These platforms provide up-to-date information on upcoming airdrops, including details on the tokens being distributed, eligibility requirements, and how to participate. They may also provide additional resources and tools to help users manage their airdropped tokens, such as portfolio trackers or exchange integrations.

Overall, airdrop platforms can be a useful tool for discovering and participating in airdrops. However, it's important to exercise caution and do your due diligence to ensure that you're participating in legitimate airdrops and protecting your personal information.

Best platforms for finding airdrops

There are many platforms that offer information about airdrops, but not all of them are equally reliable or effective. Some of the best platforms for finding airdrops include:

Airdrop Alert: Airdrop Alert is a popular platform that provides information on the latest and most promising airdrops in the market. The platform also provides tools for tracking airdrops and participating in them.

Airdrop Bob: Airdrop Bob is a platform that provides information on both ongoing and upcoming airdrops. The platform also offers reviews and ratings for different airdrops to help users make informed decisions.

Airdrops.io: Airdrops.io is another popular platform that provides information on the latest airdrops in the market. The platform also provides tools for tracking airdrops and participating in them.

CoinMarketCap: CoinMarketCap is a popular cryptocurrency market tracking platform that also provides information on airdrops. The platform offers a dedicated section for airdrops where users can find information on ongoing and upcoming airdrops.

Reddit: Reddit is a popular social media platform that has dedicated subreddits for airdrops. These subreddits provide information on the latest airdrops, as well as reviews and discussions on different airdrops.

It is important to note that while these platforms can provide useful information on airdrops, it is always advisable to do your own research and due diligence before participating in any airdrop.

There are many platforms available: While some of the most popular platforms for finding airdrops include Airdrop Alert, Airdrop Bob, and Airdrops.io, there are many other platforms available that can help you find airdrops that may not be listed on these larger platforms. It can be worthwhile to do some research to find additional platforms that fit your needs.

Not all airdrops are created equal: While airdrops can be a great way to earn free tokens, not all airdrops are worth the effort. Some airdrops may require you to complete extensive tasks, while others may not be very valuable. It's important to do your own research to determine which airdrops are worth your time and effort.

Be aware of scams: Unfortunately, there are many scams in the world of airdrops, and it's important to be aware of this. Be cautious when sharing your personal information, and never send any cryptocurrency or money to someone claiming to offer an airdrop.

Stay up-to-date: The world of cryptocurrency and airdrops is constantly changing, and it's important to stay up-to-date on the latest news and trends. Follow trusted sources on social media and sign up for newsletters to stay informed.

Use multiple platforms: While some platforms may list more airdrops than others, it can be helpful to use multiple platforms to increase your chances of finding valuable airdrops. Additionally, some platforms may offer exclusive airdrops that are not available elsewhere.

Platform reviews and comparisons

Platform reviews and comparisons are essential tools for investors and traders in the cryptocurrency market. With hundreds of different platforms available, it can be challenging to find the right one that fits your investment strategy and goals. Platform reviews and comparisons provide insights into the features, fees, security, and ease of use of various platforms, helping investors make informed decisions.

Many people do not know that platform reviews and comparisons can vary in their objectivity and accuracy. Some reviewers may have biases or receive compensation for promoting specific platforms, leading to potentially misleading reviews. Therefore, it's essential to do your own research and seek out multiple reviews from reputable sources before making any decisions.

Another important aspect of platform reviews and comparisons is the need to consider your own preferences and needs. Not all platforms are created equal, and what works for one investor may not work for another. Factors such as user interface, customer support, and available assets should be considered when evaluating different platforms.

It's also important to note that the cryptocurrency market is constantly evolving, and new platforms and features are emerging regularly. Therefore, it's a good idea to regularly revisit platform reviews and comparisons to stay up to date on the latest developments and ensure that you are still using the best platform for your needs.

When it comes to platform reviews and comparisons for airdrops, it's important to do your research and consider a variety of factors. Here are some things that people may not know about this topic:

Trustworthiness of the platform: It's important to research the platform's history and reputation before using it. Look for reviews from other users and check if there have been any security issues or scams associated with the platform.

Quality of the airdrops: Not all airdrops are created equal, and some may not be worth the effort. Look for platforms that offer high-quality airdrops from reputable projects with real-world use cases.

User experience: Some platforms may have a confusing or difficult-to-use interface, making it challenging to navigate and participate in airdrops. Look for platforms with a user-friendly design and clear instructions for participation.

Availability of customer support: If you have any questions or issues with airdrops, it's helpful to have access to customer support. Look for platforms that offer responsive customer support, preferably with multiple channels for communication.

Fees and costs: Some platforms may charge fees for participating in airdrops or withdrawing tokens. Consider the fees associated with using the platform and whether they are reasonable.

Geographic restrictions: Some airdrops may only be available to users in certain geographic regions. Look for platforms that offer a variety of airdrops and are not limited by geographic restrictions.

Compatibility with your wallet or exchange: Make sure the platform is compatible with your preferred wallet or exchange to ensure a smooth process for receiving and trading your airdropped tokens.

By considering these factors and doing your research, you can find the best platform for your needs and maximize your chances of receiving high-quality airdrops.

How to spot fake airdrop platforms

As the popularity of airdrops has increased, so has the number of fake airdrop platforms. These platforms are designed to scam unsuspecting users and trick them into giving away their private keys, passwords, or other sensitive information. Here are some tips to help you spot fake airdrop platforms:

Check the website URL: Scammers often use URLs that are similar to the legitimate platform's URL but with slight differences. Check the URL carefully to ensure that it is the correct one.

Look for the lock icon: Always make sure that the website has a lock icon in the address bar, indicating that it is using HTTPS encryption.

Check the social media pages: Legitimate airdrop platforms will have active social media pages, so check their profiles on Twitter, Telegram, and other social media platforms to see if they are active and have a significant following.

Research the team behind the platform: Check the team's background, qualifications, and experience. Legitimate platforms will have a team that is easily verifiable and will provide complete information about themselves.

Be cautious of high rewards: If the airdrop offers a reward that seems too good to be true, it probably is. Legitimate platforms will offer reasonable rewards that are in line with the market value of the token.

Don't give away your private key or password: Legitimate platforms will never ask for your private key or password. If a platform asks for this information, it is likely a scam.

Use trusted sources to find airdrops: Stick to reputable sources to find airdrops, such as established airdrop platforms, cryptocurrency news sites, or official social media pages of the projects themselves.

By following these tips, you can protect yourself from falling victim to fake airdrop platforms and keep your cryptocurrency investments safe.

How to avoid scams

Airdrops can be a great way to earn free tokens, but unfortunately, there are many scams out there. Here are some tips on how to avoid airdrop scams:

Do your research: Before participating in an airdrop, research the project and team behind it. Look for information about the project's whitepaper, roadmap, and team members. If there is little to no information available, or if the information seems sketchy, it's best to steer clear.

Check the website's security: Make sure the website you're visiting is secure by checking for "https" in the URL and looking for the padlock icon in your browser's address bar.

Don't give away personal information: Legitimate airdrops typically do not require personal information such as your social security number, passport number, or bank account information. Be wary of airdrops that ask for this type of information.

Beware of phishing scams: Scammers may try to trick you into giving away your private keys by creating fake airdrop websites or sending phishing emails. Always double-check the URL and sender's email address before entering any information or clicking on any links.

Use reputable airdrop platforms: Stick to using well-known and reputable airdrop platforms to avoid falling victim to a scam. Read reviews and do your due diligence before signing up for any platform.

Be skeptical of large rewards: If an airdrop is offering a large amount of tokens for little to no effort on your part, it's likely too good to be true. Use caution and do your research before participating in such airdrops.

Use anti-virus software: Make sure your computer is protected with up-to-date anti-virus software to help detect and prevent scams.

Remember, if something seems too good to be true, it probably is. Use caution, do your research, and always protect your personal information.

Here are some additional tips on how to avoid scams related to airdrops:

Research the project: Before participating in an airdrop, it's important to do your due diligence and research the project. Check the project's website, whitepaper, and social media channels to ensure it's legitimate and has a solid team and product.

Beware of fake social media accounts: Scammers may create fake social media accounts for the project to trick users into sending them money or personal information. Verify the authenticity of the social media accounts by checking for the blue checkmark or by contacting the official project team.

Never send money or personal information: Legitimate airdrops will never ask you to send money or personal information. If you're asked to do so, it's likely a scam.

Use reputable airdrop platforms: Stick to using reputable airdrop platforms and avoid clicking on links from unknown sources.

Be wary of high reward airdrops: If an airdrop promises an unusually high reward, it's likely too good to be true and may be a scam.

Trust your instincts: If something feels off or too good to be true, trust your instincts and avoid participating in the airdrop.

Check for reviews and feedback: Look for reviews and feedback from other users who have participated in the airdrop to gauge its legitimacy.

By taking these steps and staying vigilant, you can avoid falling victim to airdrop scams and protect yourself and your assets.

PART 5
Advanced Airdrop Strategies

CHAPTER 8
ADVANCED AIRDROP STRATEGIES

Advanced airdrop strategies can help investors maximize their rewards from airdrops. Here are some strategies that many people may not know of:

Airdrop farming: This strategy involves actively seeking out airdrops from new and upcoming projects that have high potential for growth. This requires regular monitoring of social media, forums, and news outlets for new project announcements.

Holding airdropped tokens

Instead of selling airdropped tokens immediately, holding them for a longer period may result in greater profits if the project succeeds. This strategy is often used by long-term investors who are willing to take on higher risks for potentially higher rewards.

Holding airdropped tokens can be a lucrative strategy for investors who believe in the long-term potential of the project. By holding onto the tokens, investors can potentially benefit from price appreciation if the project becomes successful.

One thing many people may not know is that holding airdropped tokens can also come with certain risks. For example, if the tokens are held in a centralized exchange, they may be subject to hacking or other security risks. Similarly, if the tokens are held in a wallet with private keys that are lost or stolen, the tokens may be permanently inaccessible.

To mitigate these risks, investors may want to consider holding their airdropped tokens in a secure hardware wallet, which can provide an extra layer of security. They should also take care to backup their private keys and keep them in a safe place, and avoid sharing them with anyone.

Another important consideration when holding airdropped tokens is the tax implications. Depending on the country and tax laws, holding tokens for a certain period of time may be subject to capital gains taxes when they are sold. Investors should consult with a tax professional to understand their specific tax obligations.

Overall, holding airdropped tokens can be a valuable strategy for investors who are willing to take on the associated risks and are confident in the long-term potential of the project. However, it's important to approach holding airdropped tokens with caution and to take steps to mitigate risks such as using secure wallets and consulting with tax professionals.

Holding airdropped tokens can be a good way to diversify your portfolio and potentially earn a profit if the value of the tokens increases over time. Here are some things to keep in mind when holding airdropped tokens:

Do your research: Before holding any airdropped tokens, make sure you do your due diligence and research the project behind the tokens. Look at their whitepaper, team members, partnerships, and any other relevant information. This will help you make an informed decision about whether or not to hold the tokens.

Monitor the market: Keep an eye on the market and the price of the tokens you are holding. Use tools like CoinMarketCap or

CoinGecko to track the price and volume of the tokens. This will help you make informed decisions about whether to hold, sell, or trade the tokens.

Stay up to date: Keep up to date with news and updates about the project behind the tokens you are holding. Follow their social media channels, join their community groups, and sign up for their newsletters. This will help you stay informed about any changes or developments that may affect the value of the tokens.

Consider selling or trading: If the value of the tokens increases significantly, you may want to consider selling or trading them. This can help you realize a profit and can also help you diversify your portfolio further.

Consider staking

Some airdropped tokens may offer staking opportunities, which can help you earn additional tokens over time. This can be a good way to earn a passive income and increase your holdings.

Staking is a process of holding a cryptocurrency in a wallet to support the security and functionality of a blockchain network. In exchange for staking their tokens, participants receive rewards in the form of additional tokens, similar to earning interest on a savings account.

In the context of airdrops, staking can be a useful strategy for maximizing the value of airdropped tokens. Many blockchain projects require users to hold a certain amount of tokens and stake them in order to participate in certain governance activities or earn additional rewards. By staking the airdropped tokens, users can potentially earn even more tokens or increase their influence in the project's decision-making process.

However, it's important to note that staking involves locking up the tokens for a certain period of time, which can limit liquidity and the ability to sell the tokens on the open market. Additionally, staking usually requires technical knowledge and access to specialized wallets or exchanges that support staking.

Before considering staking as an advanced airdrop strategy, it's important to carefully research the project's staking requirements, rewards, and risks, as well as to understand the technical aspects of staking and the potential impact on the overall investment portfolio.

Staking is a process where a user holds a certain amount of cryptocurrency in a wallet to support the operations of a blockchain network. In exchange for staking, users earn rewards in the form of more cryptocurrency. Many blockchain networks use staking as a way to secure their network and incentivize users to hold their cryptocurrency.

One way to maximize the value of your airdropped tokens is to consider staking them. By staking, you not only earn rewards, but you also help support the operations of the network. Staking can also help to reduce the overall supply of the token in circulation, which can increase its value.

However, it's important to note that staking often comes with certain requirements or risks, such as a minimum amount of tokens needed to stake, a lock-up period where the tokens cannot be moved, or potential penalties for breaking the staking agreement. It's important to do your research and understand the terms and risks associated with staking before committing your tokens.

Additionally, some airdropped tokens may not have staking functionality or may have limited staking options, so it's important to research and understand the specific token and network before considering staking as a strategy.

Remember, holding airdropped tokens carries risks, and it's important to do your research and make informed decisions. Always be cautious and don't invest more than you can afford to lose.

Participating in referral programs: Some airdrops offer referral bonuses for every new user that signs up through a referral link. By promoting the airdrop and referring others, investors can earn additional rewards.

Joining early: Some airdrops offer greater rewards to early adopters who join the airdrop during the initial stages. Joining early can also help investors avoid the risk of missing out on the airdrop altogether.

Utilizing social media platforms: Social media platforms like Twitter, Telegram, and Discord are often used to distribute information about airdrops. By following relevant accounts and participating in discussions, investors can learn about new airdrops and increase their chances of being eligible.

Participating in staking and governance: Some airdrops offer additional rewards for staking or participating in governance activities. By holding a certain amount of tokens and participating in activities like voting or proposing changes, investors can earn additional rewards and help shape the project's development.

It is important to note that advanced airdrop strategies involve higher risks and require more time and effort. Investors should conduct thorough research and carefully consider the potential risks and rewards before implementing any of these strategies.

Airdrop Arbitrage

This strategy involves taking advantage of the difference in value between the airdropped token and other cryptocurrencies. For instance, if a token is airdropped at a value of $1, but is worth $2 on a cryptocurrency exchange, you can sell it on the exchange and make a profit.

Airdrop arbitrage is a strategy that involves taking advantage of price discrepancies in airdropped tokens across different exchanges. The idea is to receive the tokens through an airdrop and then sell them immediately on an exchange where they are trading at a higher price. This can potentially result in quick profits without having to invest any money into buying the tokens.

To engage in airdrop arbitrage, it's important to keep an eye on multiple exchanges and monitor the prices of the airdropped tokens.

It's also important to be aware of any trading fees and transfer fees that may eat into potential profits.

However, it's worth noting that airdrop arbitrage can be risky, as prices can be volatile and unpredictable. Additionally, there may be restrictions on when and how airdropped tokens can be sold, and some exchanges may have low liquidity or trading volume for certain tokens.

It's also important to note that airdrop arbitrage is not guaranteed to be profitable, and should be approached with caution and careful consideration. It's important to thoroughly research the tokens and exchanges involved, and to have a solid understanding of the risks involved.

Airdrop arbitrage is a strategy that involves exploiting the price difference between the value of the airdropped tokens and their market price. The idea is to claim the airdrop tokens and then sell them on an exchange at a higher price, thereby making a profit.

One way to approach airdrop arbitrage is to identify new or lesser-known tokens that have a high airdrop value, but are not yet listed on major exchanges. The value of these tokens may be lower because there is less demand for them on the market, but their airdrop value may be high due to the need to create awareness and build a user base.

To make the most of airdrop arbitrage, you need to act quickly and have access to reliable information. Keep an eye on airdrop news and announcements, and be prepared to claim airdrops as soon as they become available. You can also use social media and community channels to stay up-to-date on new airdrops and emerging tokens.

It is worth noting that airdrop arbitrage is not risk-free, as the value of the tokens can be volatile and there is no guarantee that their market value will increase. Additionally, some airdrops may require you to hold the tokens for a certain period of time, which can limit your ability to sell them immediately.

Overall, airdrop arbitrage can be a profitable strategy for those who are willing to take on the risks and do their research.

Airdrop Farming

This strategy involves signing up for multiple airdrops and holding onto the tokens until they increase in value. This can be a risky strategy since not all tokens may increase in value, but it can also be a way to potentially earn significant profits.

Airdrop farming is a practice where individuals or groups try to maximize their profits by participating in as many airdrops as possible, often using multiple accounts or different methods to bypass restrictions. While it is not illegal, it is considered an unethical practice by many, as it often goes against the intended purpose of airdrops and can create unfair advantages for a few individuals at the expense of others.

Airdrop farming usually involves using multiple email addresses, social media accounts, and other means to register for the same airdrop multiple times. This allows the farmer to receive more tokens than they would otherwise be eligible for, which they can then sell on the market or use for other purposes.

Some airdrop farmers also use bots or automation tools to automate the registration process, which can increase their chances of receiving airdrops and reduce the amount of time they spend on manual registration.

While airdrop farming can be profitable for those who engage in it, it can also harm the overall health of the cryptocurrency ecosystem by distorting token prices and creating unfair advantages for a few individuals. As a result, many airdrop platforms have implemented measures to prevent or discourage airdrop farming, such as limiting the number of accounts or tokens that can be received per individual.

I'm sorry, but there is no legitimate strategy or practice called "airdrop farming." This term may be used by scammers or fraudsters to trick people into giving away their personal information or cryptocurrency. It's important to be cautious and skeptical of any scheme or offer that promises free or easy profits, as there is often a catch or risk involved. It's always recommended to do thorough research and consult with trusted sources before participating in any investment or cryptocurrency-related activity.

Airdrop Flipping: This strategy involves quickly selling the airdropped tokens for a profit. This requires a bit of skill and timing, as you need to sell the tokens before their value drops.

Referral Airdrops: Many airdrops offer additional tokens if you refer others to the airdrop. By referring as many people as possible, you can earn more tokens for yourself.

Token Swapping

Some airdrops may offer a token swap, where you can exchange your airdropped tokens for other cryptocurrencies or tokens. This can be a way to diversify your holdings and potentially increase your profits.

Token swapping, also known as token trading or exchanging, is the process of exchanging one type of cryptocurrency or token for another. In the context of airdrops, token swapping can be used to convert airdropped tokens into another cryptocurrency or token, which can be more widely used or traded on various exchanges.

One thing many people may not know about token swapping is that it can be done on both centralized and decentralized exchanges. Centralized exchanges are run by a central authority, which can be a company or a group of individuals. Decentralized exchanges, on the other hand, are peer-to-peer networks that allow users to trade directly with one another without the need for a central authority.

Another thing to consider when swapping airdropped tokens is the fees involved. Some exchanges charge high fees for token swaps, while others may have lower fees or even no fees at all. It's important to do your research and compare different exchanges to find the best option for your needs.

It's also worth noting that token swapping can be risky, especially when dealing with new or unknown tokens. Before swapping any tokens, it's important to do your due diligence and research the token's team, technology, and potential use cases. It's also a good idea to start with small amounts and gradually increase your investment as you become more comfortable with the process.

Token swapping is a popular way to trade or exchange one cryptocurrency for another without going through the hassle of using a traditional exchange. This is made possible by decentralized exchanges (DEXs) such as Uniswap, PancakeSwap, and SushiSwap, which operate on a peer-to-peer basis without any intermediaries.

One common strategy for token swapping is to trade airdropped tokens for more established cryptocurrencies, such as Bitcoin or Ethereum, which can then be used to purchase other assets or simply held as a store of value. This allows airdrop recipients to convert their tokens into more liquid and widely accepted cryptocurrencies, potentially increasing their value over time.

Another strategy is to use token swapping to take advantage of arbitrage opportunities between different exchanges. This involves buying a cryptocurrency on one exchange where it is priced lower, then immediately selling it on another exchange where it is priced higher. This can be done using a decentralized exchange like Uniswap, which allows for fast and low-cost trades without needing to go through the traditional banking system.

It's important to note, however, that token swapping can carry risks, including volatility, liquidity issues, and potential security concerns. It's important to do your own research and carefully consider the risks and benefits before engaging in any token swapping activities.

It's important to note that these advanced strategies come with increased risk and require careful consideration before investing time and resources. It's also important to always do your own research and due diligence before participating in any airdrops or cryptocurrency-related activities.

CHAPTER 9
HOW TO CREATE YOUR OWN AIRDROPS

Creating your own airdrop can be a way to promote your project or cryptocurrency, as well as distribute tokens to potential users or investors. Here are some things many people may not know about creating their own airdrop:

Choose the right platform: There are several platforms that can be used to create an airdrop, such as Airdrop Alert, Airdrops.io, and Airdrop King. Each platform has its own requirements, fees, and benefits, so it is important to choose the right one for your needs.

Define your goals: Before creating an airdrop, it is important to define your goals. Do you want to increase awareness of your project, attract new users or investors, or reward existing ones? Having clear goals will help you create an airdrop that is effective and meets your needs.

Set eligibility criteria: To ensure that your airdrop is distributed to the right people, you should set eligibility criteria. For example, you may require participants to follow your project on social media or join your Telegram group. You can also set requirements based on location, age, or other factors.

Choose the right tokens: When creating an airdrop, you need to choose the right tokens to distribute. You can distribute your own cryptocurrency or partner with other projects to distribute their tokens. It is important to choose tokens that have value and are likely to attract participants.

Plan your distribution strategy: Once you have created your airdrop, you need to plan your distribution strategy. You can promote your airdrop on social media, forums, and other channels to attract participants. You can also partner with other projects to promote your airdrop to their communities.

Monitor and analyze results: After your airdrop is launched, it is important to monitor and analyze the results. You can track the number of participants, engagement rates, and other metrics to see how effective your airdrop is. This will help you make changes and improve future airdrops.

Compliance: When creating your own airdrop, it is important to ensure that you comply with relevant laws and regulations. This may include KYC (know your customer) requirements, anti-money laundering regulations, and securities laws. It is important to consult with legal and regulatory experts to ensure that your airdrop is compliant.

Creating your own airdrops can be a great way to promote your project, build a community, and reward early supporters. However, there are several things to consider before launching your own airdrop.

First, you need to determine the purpose of your airdrop. Are you trying to build awareness for your project or reward your existing community? Are you looking to attract new users or investors? The answers to these questions will help you determine the size and type of airdrop you want to offer.

Once you have defined the purpose of your airdrop, you need to decide on the type of tokens you will be airdropping. Will it be a new token that you have created specifically for this purpose, or will you be airdropping an existing token? If it's a new token, you will need to create a smart contract and decide on the token distribution method.

Next, you need to set the eligibility criteria for your airdrop. Who will be eligible to receive your airdrop? Will you require users to complete certain tasks or meet specific criteria? You should also consider how you will verify eligibility and prevent fraud.

Once you have defined the eligibility criteria, you can start promoting your airdrop. Social media platforms and crypto communities can be great places to promote your airdrop. You can also consider partnering with influencers or running targeted advertising campaigns to increase visibility.

Finally, you need to distribute your airdropped tokens. Depending on the size and scope of your airdrop, you may choose to distribute tokens manually or through an automated system. It's important to ensure that the distribution process is secure, transparent, and fair.

Overall, creating your own airdrops can be a powerful tool for promoting your project and building your community. However, it's important to carefully consider the purpose, type, eligibility criteria, promotion, and distribution of your airdrop to ensure its success.

How to participate in bounty programs

Bounty programs are another way to earn cryptocurrency or tokens by completing certain tasks or promoting a project. Here are some tips to maximize your chances of success when participating in bounty programs:

Choose the right projects: Look for bounty programs of projects that you believe in and that have a strong potential for growth. This will help keep you motivated and increase your chances of earning rewards.

Read the rules carefully: Each bounty program will have its own rules and requirements. Make sure to read them carefully and follow them closely. Failure to follow the rules can result in disqualification from the program.

Create quality content: If the bounty program requires you to create content such as blog posts, videos, or social media posts, make sure to create high-quality content that is relevant and engaging. This will increase your chances of getting noticed by the project team and earning rewards.

Be active on social media: Many bounty programs require you to be active on social media and promote the project. Make sure to engage with the community and share high-quality content that is relevant to the project.

Stay organized: Keep track of the tasks you need to complete and the deadlines for each task. This will help you stay on track and ensure that you don't miss any important deadlines.

Be patient: Bounty programs can take time to pay out rewards. Make sure to be patient and wait for the project team to verify your work and distribute rewards.

Beware of scams: Like with airdrops, there are also scams in the bounty program space. Make sure to do your research and only participate in reputable programs.

Overall, participating in bounty programs can be a great way to earn cryptocurrency or tokens, but it requires effort and dedication. By following these tips, you can increase your chances of success and earn rewards for your hard work.

Here are some additional tips for participating in bounty programs:

Choose the right bounty program: Before participating in a bounty program, it's important to do your research and choose the right one. Look for programs that offer rewards in a cryptocurrency that has potential for growth and has a strong community backing it.

Read the rules carefully: Make sure you read the rules and requirements of the bounty program carefully. Some programs may require specific tasks to be completed in order to qualify for rewards, so it's important to understand what is expected of you before you begin.

Be consistent: Consistency is key when participating in bounty programs. Make a schedule and stick to it, so that you can complete tasks in a timely manner and earn the maximum amount of rewards.

Stay organized: Keeping track of your progress and the tasks you have completed can help you stay organized and ensure that you don't miss out on any rewards.

Be creative: Many bounty programs require participants to create content such as articles, videos, or social media posts. Being creative and standing out from the crowd can help you earn more rewards and increase your chances of being selected for special bonuses.

Engage with the community: Engaging with the community and building relationships with other participants can help you stay motivated and learn more about the cryptocurrency ecosystem. It can also increase your chances of being selected for special bonuses or rewards.

Stay up to date: Make sure you stay up to date with the latest news and updates regarding the cryptocurrency project that you are participating in. This can help you create more relevant and engaging content, and increase your chances of earning rewards.

Be patient: Some bounty programs may take weeks or even months to complete, so it's important to be patient and persistent. Don't give up if you don't see immediate results, and keep working towards your goals.

How to use airdrops for marketing

Airdrops can be a powerful tool for marketing your cryptocurrency project. By distributing tokens for free to a large number of users, you can generate interest and awareness for your project, as well as incentivize early adoption and usage.

Here are some tips for using airdrops for marketing:

Define your target audience: Before launching an airdrop, it's important to identify your target audience. This will help you tailor your airdrop to appeal to the right users and maximize its impact. For example, if you're launching a decentralized finance (DeFi) project, you may want to target users who are interested in DeFi and have a history of using similar products.

Set clear goals: It's important to have clear goals for your airdrop, such as increasing user adoption or generating social media buzz. This will help you measure the success of your campaign and make adjustments as needed.

Choose the right distribution channels: There are many different ways to distribute airdrops, from social media campaigns to community forums to specialized airdrop platforms. Choose the channels that are most likely to reach your target audience and align with your goals.

Create a compelling offer: To incentivize users to participate in your airdrop, you'll need to create a compelling offer. This could be a large token allocation, an exclusive bonus, or a chance to win additional tokens by referring friends.

Leverage social media: Social media platforms like Twitter and Telegram can be powerful tools for promoting your airdrop and engaging with users. Consider creating a dedicated social media account for your project and using paid advertising to reach a wider audience.

Monitor the results: Once your airdrop is underway, it's important to monitor the results and make adjustments as needed. This may involve tweaking your distribution channels, adjusting your offer, or targeting different user groups.

By following these tips, you can use airdrops to build awareness, incentivize adoption, and drive user engagement for your cryptocurrency project.

Airdrops are generally used for marketing purposes, as they help spread awareness of a new token or project. However, there are other ways that airdrops can be used for marketing. Here are some additional strategies:

Targeted airdrops: Instead of a general airdrop, you can target specific communities or individuals who are likely to be interested in your project. This can help you reach your ideal audience more effectively.

Referral programs: You can encourage people to share your airdrop with their friends and followers by offering a referral bonus. This can help your airdrop go viral and reach a larger audience.

Social media promotions: You can use social media platforms like Twitter, Facebook, and Instagram to promote your airdrop and reach a wider audience. You can also partner with influencers or crypto enthusiasts to help spread the word.

Community engagement: Engage with your community and encourage them to participate in your airdrop. This can help build a strong community around your project and create a sense of loyalty among your supporters.

Partnership airdrops: Partner with other projects or companies in the space to offer joint airdrops. This can help you reach new audiences and build relationships with other players in the industry.

Overall, airdrops can be a powerful tool for marketing your project, but it's important to use them strategically and thoughtfully to get the best results.

How to invest in airdrop projects

Investing in airdrop projects can be a way to profit from the tokens distributed through airdrops. Here are some tips on how to invest in airdrop projects:

Do your research: Just like with any other investment, it's important to do your due diligence and research the project before investing. Look into the team, the technology, the roadmap, and any partnerships or collaborations the project may have.

Look for promising projects: Airdrop projects that have a strong team, a clear vision, and a solid plan for development and growth are more likely to be successful in the long term. Look for projects that have a clear use case and solve a real problem in the market.

Pay attention to the airdrop details: When considering investing in an airdrop project, pay attention to the details of the airdrop itself. How many tokens are being distributed? What is the distribution method? What is the vesting period for the tokens?

Consider the token economics: It's important to understand the token economics of the project, including the total supply of tokens, the circulating supply, and the inflation rate. This information can give you an idea of the potential value of the tokens over time.

Evaluate the market demand: Look at the current market demand for the token and consider the potential demand in the future. A token that has a strong use case and is in demand will likely have a higher value over time.

Manage risk: As with any investment, it's important to manage your risk. Only invest what you can afford to lose, and consider diversifying your portfolio across multiple projects and asset classes.

Stay up-to-date: Keep up-to-date with news and developments related to the project, as well as any changes to the airdrop or token distribution. This can help you make informed decisions about when to buy or sell your tokens.

It's important to remember that investing in airdrop projects can be risky, and there is no guarantee of returns. However, with careful research and analysis, it is possible to identify promising projects and potentially profit from their tokens.

Here are some additional points to consider when investing in airdrop projects:

Research the project thoroughly: Before investing in any airdrop project, it's essential to do your own research and analysis. Look into the project's team, technology, tokenomics, and community to assess its potential for success.

Check the credibility of the team: Verify the credibility and expertise of the project's team members to ensure they have the necessary skills and experience to execute the project successfully.

Analyze the tokenomics: Analyze the tokenomics of the project to understand how the tokens will be used and distributed. This includes understanding the supply, distribution, and circulation of tokens.

Monitor the market: Keep an eye on the market trends and analyze how the airdrop project is performing in the market. This will help you make informed decisions about when to buy, hold, or sell your tokens.

Diversify your portfolio: Don't put all your investment in one airdrop project. Instead, diversify your portfolio by investing in multiple projects to reduce your risk exposure.

Watch out for scams: Be cautious of airdrop projects that promise high returns with little to no effort. Such projects are often scams, and you can lose your investment.

Seek professional advice: Consider seeking professional advice from financial advisors or investment managers to help you make informed decisions about investing in airdrop projects.

Investing in airdrop projects can be a risky venture, but it can also be a profitable one if you make informed decisions and invest wisely.

www.ingramcontent.com/pod-product-compliance
Lightning Source LLC
Chambersburg PA
CBHW031532210526
45464CB00015B/824